INSTITUTIONALIZING INNOVATION

INSTITUTIONALIZING INNOVATION

A STUDY OF ORGANIZATIONAL LEARNING SYSTEMS

MARIANN JELINEK

PRAEGER PUBLISHERS
Praeger Special Studies

New York　　•　　London　　•　　Sydney　　•　　Toronto

Library of Congress Cataloging in Publication Data

Jelinek, Mariann.
    Institutionalizing innovation.

    Bibliography: p.
    Includes index.
    1. Technological innovations. 2. Industrial
management. I. Title.
HD45.J38 1979   658.4'06   78-25708
ISBN 0-03-047031-5

PRAEGER PUBLISHERS,

PRAEGER SPECIAL STUDIES

383 Madison Avenue, New York, N.Y. 10017, U.S.A.

Published in the United States of America in 1979
by Praeger Publishers, Inc.
A Division of Holt, Rinehart and Winston, CBS, Inc.

9   038   987654321

Printed in the United States of America

To
J. A. and M. E. L.
for
"the spice in my life."

PREFACE

This study began with a personal quandary. The literature suggested that organizations didn't "learn" in any meaningful sense, and didn't plan in any way that mattered. Yet some organizations certainly did seem to change and grow and innovate, while others did not. It didn't seem reasonable that it was purely a matter of luck. The quandary was deepened further when Patrick E. Haggerty of Texas Instruments (TI) described his company. TI, it seemed, not only succeeded, grew, changed, and planned; it also went about these processes systematically. TI even had a formal system for developing new ideas into products, integrated with the day-to-day management of the firm. All this suggested that TI had created a learning system, something not described in any of the literature.

Mr. Haggerty's kind assistance made possible the field research on which this study is based. The data gathered in Texas was only part of the story, however. Only in the context of evolving techniques of management did the meaning come clear. TI had evolved a next step in organizational controls, one adaptable and applicable to strategic innovation. Strategic innovation, by its nature, is a highly uncertain matter. Thus the problem of guiding and controlling innovation is peculiarly difficult. TI's practices built the successful approaches of past innovation into a systematic (and controllable) format. The OST (Objectives, Strategies and Tactics) System generalized from successful *practice*; it was empirically based upon what had worked. To understand it, however, a theoretical structure was required to demonstrate just what the evolutionary step was that TI had made. That framework is presented here.

TI's OST System is not just the practices of Patrick E. Haggerty. Indeed, the "proof of the pudding" lies in the system's development beyond what Haggerty envisioned. Further evolution of the system to meet changed conditions and to incorporate the new insights of others who grew up, as managers, within the OST, rendered it independent, even of its creator. That is, because the system can be polished, shaped, and changed by others, it represents truly organizational learning—not simply the knowledge or learning of any single individual. The story of the OST's evolution is also presented here, at least in its early stages. The system is still evolving.

A Preface is the traditional place to record acknowledgments: this one shall be no exception. A first and most obvious debt is to Patrick E. Haggerty. He provided both an idea and my first exposure to an operational integrated planning system. I am grateful as well both for his generous gift of his own scarce time, and for the opportunity to meet a contemplative mover and doer. Without his help, this study would not have come to pass.

The dissertation that forms the basis for this book benefited enormously from the encouragement, persistence, and high standards of intellectual excellence held forth by the members of my committee: Chairman Paul R. Lawrence, Richard F. Vancil, and Charles J. Christenson, all of the Graduate School of Business Administration, Harvard University. The give-and-take and stimulus of discourse with them helped to shape my thoughts. Professor Alfred D. Chandler, Jr., also of the Harvard Business School, provided the inspiration for attempting an historical approach. His comments made many complex ideas clear and familiar. His assistance and encouragement were invaluable. Professor Joseph A. Litterer of the University of Massachusetts at Amherst challenged my thinking, and cheered my efforts to try something well beyond my initial grasp. His encouragement, sharp questioning, and high standards are deeply appreciated. To each of these I might say, "Without you, it wouldn't have happened." Their aid is gratefully acknowledged, although of course the responsibility for any shortcomings must be my own.

The drawings were done by Marie Litterer.

Mariann Jelinek
Cornish, New Hampshire

CONTENTS

LIST OF TABLES AND FIGURES

INTRODUCTION

THE PROBLEM AND THE PRESENT STATE OF THEORY

How does an organization "learn"? That is, how does a coordinated enterprise generate new "official" responses to environmental changes that go beyond simple stimulus-response adaptation, to impound the results of experience into new routines, or to generalize from one new experience to others? It is clear that some organizations respond more effectively to changing environments than others: some survive, while others do not. We say that some are more innovative than others. And we frequently allude to the need for more flexibility in modern business and government. Indeed, it is a truism to remark nowadays that technology and social change have created a "turbulent environment," as Emery and Trist call it,[1] for business especially. Even old and well-established industries face major changes (like the Pilkington float glass process, EEO, consumerism, new technologies, or pollution controls). Even governments are confronted with the impact of data processing, mass media, and organized client dissent—to say nothing of the interconnected results of seemingly disparate actions or events.

At the same time, there is an increasing concern over the failure of innovation in U.S. industry (to ignore government and nonprofit organizations). Thus in its January 15, 1972 issue, *Business Week* sought to aid managers in "Making U.S. Technology More Competitive." In the April, 1972 issue of *Fortune*, a major article addressed "Why the U.S. Lags in Technology." On February 16, 1976, *Business Week* again carried a cover article lamenting "The Breakdown of U.S. Innovation." "No-risk Supercautious Management" which is also called "the MBA syndrome," is the culprit. On July 3, 1978, *Business Week* again addressed the problem of innovation in a feature article on America's "Vanishing Innovation." This time, the culprit was governmental policy. Nor are *Business Week* and *Fortune* alone in their concern. Jordan J. Baruch[2] has suggested that companies may find themselves faced with "technological imperatives" demanding change. In 1978, in his capacity as Assistant Commerce Secretary for Science and Technology, Baruch directed a massive, 28-agency White House policy study reviewing government's role in helping or hindering innovation. There is a sizable literature on technological change and the diffusion of technology as well, testifying to widespread interest in these topics. In a parallel vein, the literature on organizational change and organizational development is also voluminous.

Amid all the concern for change, however, there is very little theory on impounding change or change procedures as organizational learning. We have no internally consistent language for precisely discussing this. Much of the problem may be traceable to the youth of organizational theory, itself only some 75 or 85 years old. More of the problem may be traced to the hesitancy with which we develop new paradigms* for describing complex levels of organization and rates of change not intuitively obvious nor readily accessible through biological or mechanical analogies. Indeed, morphogenesis—the ability to purposively *change structure*—is a distinguishing characteristic of organizations that separates them definitively from machines or organisms, making comparative analogies logically dubious.

The need for a new conceptual model is underscored by a central ambiguity of organizational theory, memorialized in endless debates: how can we speak of an organization's "goals" and "actions" when, paradoxically, only *individuals* ever decide, act, or function as organizational members? Beneath the paradox are two truths. First, it is obvious that only people—not the corporate, legal entities—are conscious, or can purposefully act, decide, or consider. Second, organizations do "have a life of their own," the "something more"† in terms of accomplishment (frequently labeled synergy) beyond the sum of the parts that make the organization. This "something more" is the *raison d'être* for organizations in the first place. Organizations accomplish tasks beyond the abilities of their members as individuals, or even as aggregates, because of the coordination they provide.[3]

The theory of organizations, in general, suggests that organizations "learn," if at all, by some process comparable with individual learning. Usually the phrase "organizational learning" is used merely to pose a loose analogy between the individual and the organization, in modes of acquiring knowledge, in goals, in actions, or in decision making. Perhaps because of the contradictions inherent in this usage, theorists who have used the analogy have not gone beyond the figure of speech. Thus Cyert and March

---

*Thomas Kuhn has developed a theory of paradigm change in *The Structure of Scientific Revolutions*, 2nd ed. (Chicago: University of Chicago Press, 1970). Kuhn suggests that anomalies unexplainable under existing theory are discounted until a substantial number of them are collected, creating overwhelming pressure for change. A basically conservative bent protects the inadequate old theory long after some evidence has suggested that it might be incomplete.

In organization theory especially, simple mechanical or organic models have been most seductive, and most tenacious, despite substantial evidence that the analogical thinking on which they are based is misleading.

†Charles J. Christenson has pointed out that organizations can also be described as "something less" in that the coordination and programming they provide *decreases* the variability in performance that might be expected on the basis of pure chance (personal

suggest a coalitional view of organizations, noting that "the idea of an organizational goal and the conception of an organization as a coalition are implicitly contradictory."[4] However, they go on to accept the contradiction, and the paraphrastic analogy between individual and organizational goals. They then consider the genesis of "organizational goals" as a purely reactive mechanism via various methods of quasi-resolution of conflict.

Similarly with organizational learning, Cyert and March focus on short-range adaptive behavior, explicitly assuming that procedures for adjusting decision rules are "given." They assume, or choose to pass over, much of what seems to be central to a discussion of organizational learning. In part, their emphasis falls upon the balance-of-power negotiations that take place in forming coalitions; in part, their field of inquiry is limited to organizations that "devote rather little time to long-run planning (that has significance for decision making)."[5] And yet, as Cyert and March point out:

> Any organization as complex as a firm adapts to its environment at many different (but interrelated) levels. It changes its behavior in response to short-run feedback from the environment according to some fairly well-defined rules. It changes rules in response to longer-run feedback according to some more general rules, and so on. At some point in this hierarchy of rule change, we describe the rules involved as "learning" rules. By this we mean (in effect) that we will not examine the hierarchy further, although it is clear wherever we stop that we can still imagine higher-level learning rules by which the lower level learning rules are modified.[6]

In one sense, this author is interested in higher levels than those that concern Cyert and March. In another, what is needed is a general framework which will permit exploration of just those "learning rules" they take as the boundary to their inquiry, and also of the process of learning rule change. We have no map for exploring these phenomena. Moreover, the central focus of this study is the large, successful firm which devotes substantial effort to long-range planning, which, in turn, *does* have an

---

communication, 1977). The net result of this particular "something less" is, therefore, "more" (or better) performance. The problem (and the heart of my investigation) lies in maintaining this "less as more" by reducing the variance in performance without obviating the possibility of *desirable* variance (change) at some later date. If such variance could be held as potential or latent—not eliminated—an organization would be prepared for change. Moreover, if a format or procedure for acquiring knowledge—a "scientific method of exploration to discover new responses"—could be generated, realizing this potential variance would be facilitated. Thus the difficulty shifts to "building in" the newly discovered variance and replicating it. This is what I believe I have observed at Texas Instruments.

impact upon the decisions and operations of the firm. If the concern of academics and practitioners with planning has any single message, it is that firms in high change, high technology industries at least, can no longer afford the luxury of *post hoc* response to change: it is critical to attain some measure of proactiveness. This requires, in its turn, explicit attention to the processes of change and learning. At the heart of this node of issues is a question of academic credibility; unless our theorizing can be used to assist this process, our efforts are wasted. We teach a good deal about planning, policy, decision making, and so on. Is it in fact useful, or purely "academic"? Without a theory, it is difficult to do more than offer an unfalsifiable opinion on the matter.

The other side of the central paradox of organization theory suggests that only *individual persons* ever decide, act, or function as organization members. In short, this position would reject the notion that organizations can be said to "learn" in any meaningful sense. From this position, Silverman asserts that systems theory, the side of the paradox which emphasizes organizational synergy, is inherently limited:[7]

> To use the concepts of organizational needs and of a system's self-regulating activities in any way other than as a heuristic device is inadmissible since it implies that the power of thought and action may reside in social constructs—this is sometimes known as the problem of reification. On the other hand, it is doubtful whether systems theorists can offer any explanation of social change without resorting to reifications.[8]

Thus the major weakness of systems theory, according to Silverman, is that it is inadequate for describing change without falling into reification. This difficulty has been particularly apparent with regard to the concept of "organizational learning." Clearly we cannot mean that an organization has a mind capable of thought, seductive though the analogy might be. It explains nothing to simply use the phrase as an analogy, for *organizations* do not think; *people* do.

The alternative Silverman proposes rests firmly upon a view of organizations as aggregates of individuals, whose frames of reference indelibly color their perceptions. This underlying individuality makes deterministic models of organizations unsound. Silverman dismisses systems theories, including those of March and Simon, and Cyert and March, as reifying and deterministically unsound.

Silverman suggests that the action frame of reference makes more adequate sense of such organizational phenomena as goals, actions, decisions, and, most importantly, organizational change. The action frame of reference poses the individual's frame of reference as a basic causative factor. By looking to individuals and their motivations, Silverman's theory permits him to weave together diverse strands from earlier thinkers' work into a more powerful tool. Thus Selznick's observation that individual members are sometimes "recalcitrant"[9] organization tools makes good sense in Silverman's terms.

To explain the undeniable communion of interest and viewpoint which is as characteristic of organizations as their members' sometime recalcitrance, Silverman posits a "shared frame of reference," on some matters. Silverman's "shared frame of reference" is akin to the concept of organizational climate—shared perceptions or ways of looking at reality, shared values as to how things ought to be done, and the like. Silverman's emphasis, however, is on the external and individual factors shaping the frame of reference—the informal, rather than the formal; the social, rather than the administrative. This focus implicitly suggests that formal administrative systems have little relevance to organization members' actions or thought patterns.

GAPS IN THE THEORY

The available theory, whether the systems approach or the action frame of reference, seems inadequate to describe the formalized, systematic means by which organizations do influence, seek to retain, replicate, and extend the insights of individual members, especially as regards innovation. Clearly organizations do differ in their ability to influence adaptation to change. Some successes might be fortuitous, or idiosyncratic—where an entrepreneur repeatedly generates successful new ideas, for instance. But firms grow beyond the founder, the entrepreneur. This transition is frequently problematical,* but it does take place. It requires a shift from depending upon individual innovators to somehow generalizing and extending these abilities. Any single leader or entrepreneur, no matter how brilliant or successful, is necessarily limited. If a firm or organization is to continue to grow, it will ultimately surpass the ability of even the extraordinary individual to coordinate and direct it, to innovate extensively enough to maintain it.

This insight is developed in some detail with regard to management and control systems in Alfred D. Chandler, Jr.'s *Strategy and Structure*.[10] It is neither size nor age that determines the need for more formalized control procedures; it is complexity. Thus Jersey Standard, Du Pont,

---

*See Salter, 1970, and Scott, 1971 for a discussion of the stages of corporate development.

Sears, and General Motors all evolved systems to organize the flow of information and assist in its interpretation in order that the ongoing business of the firm might be controlled. This development moved to a higher level of sophistication—resting upon common controls and divisionalized structure—in response to increasing complexity in the product and process lines of the companies.

The same ideas apply to innovation, particularly in a highly technical, highly changeful industry. Diversity in product, processes, and markets demands both decentralization of the innovation process and control of it by the top management, if any meaningful policy is to be developed, implemented, or maintained. To insure replication of successful approaches, rather than depending upon the fortuitous reinvention of them, something more systematic than serendipity is required. Amid increasing and continued concern about facilitating innovation, a study, such as this, of systematic innovation seems worthy of pursuit.

THE DESIDERATA

To make use of the concept of organizational learning, the idea must be made more precise. A simple analogy won't do. On the one hand, any theoretical development must take into account Silverman's objections against determinism, as well as Weber's stricture against reification.[11] On the other, the theory must nevertheless take into account the synergy and replication toward which all organizations strive. The issues are the extension beyond an individual's insight, and the critical possibilities for elaboration and for survival of what would otherwise be purely ephemeral "shared frames of reference." It is organization or patterning, retained and institutionalized, that obviates the need for all insights and learning to be within the creative capacity of a single individual. We must, therefore, consider how organizations learn.

To discuss organizational learning adequately, several refinements of concept are essential. A distinction must be drawn between *individual* learning and *organizational* learning—there has got to be a hierarchy or cutpoint, preferably more rather than less rigorous, for delineating what constitutes transferrence or transmittal beyond an individual. By rigorous is meant conservative. It seems to be preferable to reject instances which might be organizational learning, rather than to accept instances which might not be. The difficulty lies in documenting an interface, for the reductionists are right, in part; every act of learning in an organization begins with an individual "Aha!"—though it may well have been contributed to by a number of other individuals, without whose efforts the final product would not have emerged. The phenomenon of group creativity is one aspect of organizational learning, although not its only face. The question here is, when does learning go beyond the individual "Aha!" so as to be accessible to others, so as to contribute to the synergy identified earlier as one of the critical characteristics of an organization, as opposed to a mere aggregation? For purposes of building the theory, a rough and definitive distinction is preferable; refinement can come after the basic logic has been tested.

Some cutpoints suggest themselves: what is taught to another person; what is written down; what is reduced to rule or policy; what becomes part of the ongoing procedure; what is shaped by several hands and minds. In each case, knowledge moves from what Karl Popper calls the subjective reality of World 2 to the objective reality of World 3.[12]

This is a problem in epistemology. Without getting into arguments stated far more elegantly by Popper than attempted here, the qualitative shift that moves some bit of new knowledge from the individual's "I know" to the more generally available, organizationally shared "we know," should be recognized. Predictability and replicability are two key criteria. It is essential—in making crude, definitive distinctions, at least—to demonstrate that insight goes beyond the fortuitous repetition, beyond idiosyncratic comprehension. Murray's dissertation[13] makes a useful distinction between technical learning and administrative learning which can be adapted here. "Organizational learning" may be limited to Murray's administrative learning; what is formally institutionalized.

A further clarification is needed to distinguish adequately between mere adaptation and true learning. Ashby and other cyberneticists suggest that trial-and-error, or adaptation,* is the *only* route to learning. But Ashby supposes that formerly successful programs are retained; and that higher-level goals are not adjustable, but given.

> A change of goal may be of importance in the higher functionings of the nervous system, when a *sub*-goal may be established or changed provisionally; but the situation does not occur at the fundamental level that

---

*Charles J. Christenson has suggested that this vicarious learning or adoption of others' insights is no different: "Even this is 'trial-and-error'—you have not acquired my knowledge until you have formulated it in your own way and tested it, either against me or against reality" (personal communication, 1977). However, it seems to me that this mode of "testing" is, at most, very different from the kind of exploratory testing required to discover knowledge *de novo*. It may be a purely logical testing, an individual thought-process that requires no further excursions into outside reality. More to the point for organizational purposes, perhaps, knowledge comprehended; by virtue of its communication to others, it becomes accessible to further development.

we are considering here, and we shall not consider such possibilities further.[14]

and:

It is axiomatic (for *any* Black Box when the range of its inputs is *given*) that the only way in which the nature of its contents can be elicited is by the transmission of actions through it. . . . In other words, it must proceed by trial and error.[15]

What is crucial here is that, for Ashby's adapting systems, the *only* source of knowledge about the "Black Box" environment is through experience. Thus "the process of trial and error is *necessary*, for only such a process can elicit the required information."[16]

For human beings, however, an enormous amount of knowledge is acquired via others' experience: we *adopt*, as well as adapt. For organizations, such vicarious learning is taken into the available pool of variety or perception through the interface provided by an individual organization member. Furthermore, especially for higher levels of learning, beyond what I shall refer to as mere adaptation, trial-and-error alone is insufficient—it must be abstracted and generalized. To distinguish between *mere adaptation* and *learning*, the existence in the organization of a hypothesis or theory of the environment must be documented. Now, in one sense we may say that every organization, being a set of explicitly or implicitly specified relationships among parts, and between the organization and its environment, constitutes a "theory" or a "hypothesis" of the environment. But here, as with the distinction between individual and organizational learning, some further rigor seems appropriate.

Aaron Wildavsky, in the first edition of *The Politics of the Budgetary Process* (1964),[17] suggested that budgets impound a theory of the environment, and that budgetary incrementalism (building next year's budget on this year's, and making only small adjustments year by year) were evidence of organizational learning. Ten years later, in the preface to the second edition, he was much less sanguine about that:

I would no longer assume, in the absence of direct evidence, that organizations, as distinct from individuals, actually make use of the method of successive limited approximations to move away from the worse and toward the better. Not that I doubt the essentially incremental nature of budgeting. . . . The last decade's experience with social policy, however, is enough to make anyone doubt whether agencies do, in fact, use the undoubtedly incremental moves they make to observe what happens, evaluate the consequences, and adjust their activities accordingly.[18]

So one problem is the one we've already identified, the distinction between individual and organizational learning. Wildavsky continues:

> Perhaps, after all, there is no getting away from the theory of cause and effect that relates actions to consequences. Without such a theory (what economists call a production function connecting inputs to outputs), there may be no practical way either to separate the consequences of one small act from those of countless others or, amidst the confusing welter of events, to trace them back to their origins as intentional actions.[19]

Wildavsky is asserting first, that incrementalism—trial-and-error—is not itself evidence of a theory of cause-and-effect in organizations' actions; and second, that because the consequences are unclear, there can be no learning.

Wildavsky was studying governmental budgeting: the setting of the Federal budget and the various agency budgets in the Congress. It would be difficult to imagine a more highly charged environment where, due to the excessively political nature of the interactions, cause and effect must be abundantly unclear. Moreover, for the budgetary negotiations Wildavsky examines, *process* (precisely the tradeoffs and balancings that make the link between cause and effect so unclear) is as much the purpose as are the budgets set and the programs approved. The process of budget setting is an opportunity for various constituencies to make themselves heard, and to trade strengths in one area against weaknesses in another. Important decisions may be made on the basis of events which appear to be wholly unconnected with the budget under consideration, as when the fact of 1976 being an election year determined whether an agency should get a requested appropriation. This is Emery and Trist's "Turbulent Environment" with a vengeance.

But business firms are far more limited entities (as indeed are individual agencies that submit budgets). They have identifiable, delimited constituencies, missions, goals, and technologies. Because they are special-purpose entities (rather than, as with the Federal Government, fundamentally contradictory, "process and product," all-purpose entities), their actions and the consequences of them are far more limited. This makes a simpler problem. We can factor, even as business firms do; we needn't make sense of quite everything at once. In Ashby's terms, a business faces a polystable environment, with some apparent constancies factoring and subdividing that environment. It is purpose that provides the most crucial filter or funnel, cutting down somewhat on the variety and instability that must be coped with. According to Emery and Trist[20] values provide one simplifying tool for factoring environmental complexity. Institutionalizing a point of view (and we may recall Silverman and Buckley in this context) allows an organization to deal with greater amounts of complexity, if the new scheme adequately maps the changed environment which rendered old methods obsolete in the first place. We are back to institutionalizing innovation, formalizing approaches to it, in order to insure that a new map is replicated.

Firms do factor their environments, paying attention only to what is considered "relevant." Simon's concept of bounded rationality offers a convenient label for limited intentions, limited attention, and limited responses. Firms also operate on cause-and-effect relations. As Thompson points out,[21] profit-seeking organizations rest upon the assumption of technical rationality, an instrumental relationship between cause and effect. In short, economic organizations perceive some connections between action and its consequences, and behave *as if* they operated in a rational world, of less-than-wholly interdependent subenvironments. To do this, they delineate tasks, boundaries, policies, procedures, and so on. And their success can be operationalized in terms of profits, market share, productivity, growth, turnover, and the like.

While these measures do not touch directly upon "employee satisfaction," or social value, they do offer a rough and ready approximation of how successful the firm is at what is perceived to be its task. If society disagrees, the firm will fail. If organization members disagree, turnover rates will soar; survival will at least be more difficult, less efficient. The organization that survives is more successful, in these terms, than the organization that does not—but not just over the short run. The business organization that consistently makes a profit is better fitted to a changing environment than one that does not. These measures of success can be readily documented, and success in these terms constitutes a multivariate fit between various parts of the organization and various relevant parts of the environment.

A WORD ON METHODOLOGY

Learning takes place over time. It is demonstrable only in the sequential application of generalized insights or approaches, which separates it from mere adaptation or routine iteration of what was fortuitously successful in the past. The focus of this study is upon the means by which such applications take place—the administrative systems by which an organization replicates procedure, approach, and insight—particularly with regard to innovation. Said another way, this book will explore the management technology evolving to systematize the handling of innovation. Because the evidence of change must be examined over time, this study will take a narrative, longitudinal view.

The historical perspective is doubly important in this study because of important parallels between the development of systematic techniques for the management of routine business, and the emerging techniques for managing innovation. Moreover, a fresh look at some early management theory provides a model to make the present investigation more clear, by contrast and comparison, as well as an expanded data-base against which to test ideas. The parallels are important because much of what we accept as routine now was highly innovative in the early days of General Motors or Du Pont. Hence this study will employ a historical method, making use of published accounts of earlier firms' experiences for comparison.

The purpose in drawing upon the early literature of management is neither to present a comprehensive history of management thought, nor yet a development survey. Rather, a somewhat familiar data base is required from which to construct a new model of the processes of organizational learning. Taylor and Church, Du Pont, and General Motors provide familiar examples of ways to impound knowledge and make it accessible to others. Their insights, enriched by borrowings from systems theory, information theory, and scattered musings on change and logic, will provide a familiar springboard from which to survey more recent developments.

Methodology Inside Texas Instruments

A major source of data for this study was an extensive tape-recorded interview with Patrick E. Haggerty, recently retired Chairman of the Board of Texas Instruments and the prime architect of the management systems of that company. Haggerty himself is necessarily the only source of information on his own thought-processes—on why he did something, what he had in mind at the time, the connections he saw. The danger is that over-reliance on a single source might bias this analysis. Since Haggerty spoke from memory and without notes, two issues arise: accuracy and perspective. In other words, the questions are: Was his memory accurate? and, Do others in the company see things as he does? In particular, the question is whether or not others in the company actually do *use* the OST and its sister administrative systems, or merely go through the motions.

On the ground at TI, many evidences bolstered the view that the company does, indeed, run on the OST. The vocabulary and concepts recurred continually in conversations. The forms, the planning cycle, and the processes of preparing for presentations were of great importance to all the managers interviewed. Further, the resource allocation and planning processes seem to function solely on this basis. Evaluation of managers included OST results, and success in OST activities was thought critical to promotion. The OST was not a system that was simply installed; it had evolved, changing as experience dictated, to become thoroughly institutionalized over the course of about six years. Hence an historical perspective was called for here, too. In addition, there seemed no doubt, either among the TI managers interviewed, or in the few accounts by outside analysts of the system, that Haggerty was chiefly responsible for the system and its success. The OST was, to begin with, Haggerty's thinking. It was later generalized and made accessible to others, but only after Haggerty had husbanded it through its early, lean years. Since this was so, Haggerty was a prime data source, critical to the study.

To guard against the possibility that Haggerty remembered things imperfectly, his statements published at the time the systems evolved were referred to, since several speeches, presentations, and interviews were fortunately available.

From another point of view, however, the critical question becomes: "Are the ideas Haggerty describes indeed institutionalized?" That is, are they shared *in some formal way* by others in the organization? To provide this kind of cross-validation, 17 TI managers were interviewed in depth (interviews ranged up to six hours in length). To a lesser extent, manuals and published, in-company statements describing the OST, its forms, and processes were consulted. Further "external" validation included reference to published interviews with various TI managers, both in the early days of the OST and more recently. Finally, necessarily less rigorously, I drew upon my own reading of the nuances and cues I perceived in conversation, and my observation of the attitudes and opinions in evidence around me in the field.

Building Theory

At bottom, this study is an attempt to build theory, to conceptualize "institutionalized innovation" and "organizational learning" in new ways. Because the theory is in its formative stages, the proof of it is its internal consistency, together with some validation against the reality of a single case and against the additional data of the historical record. Texas Instruments is chosed as a critical test case. A highly successful firm in a highly changeful, innovative, sophisticated, and technologically advanced industry can be expected to provide the kind of learning system for this study. Perhaps as important, the test firm's attention to its own processes provides a vocabulary as well as an empirically validated approach against which to test theory.

An adequate output from this study would include a theoretical description of an existing system, and an internally consistent framework of logic that made sense of it. The output should also facilitate articulation of the underlying concepts in a more general fashion that is *not* company-specific or idiosyncratic, by relating this system and its underlying concepts to the larger body of management theory and to the historical database. And finally, the study should result in generating hypotheses which might be testable elsewhere, to validate the theory more broadly. It should be clear that the aim here is to build the theory, rather than to test the hypotheses that will or will not corroborate it on a broad scale.

NOTES

1. F. E. Emery and E. L. Trist, "Casual Texture of Organizational Management of New Knowledge: A Case Study of a State Bureaucracy," doctoral dissertation, MIT, 1975.

2. Jordan J. Baruch, "The Management of Process Change: Lever on Productivity," mimeographed, Graduate School of Business Administration, Harvard University, 1972.

3. Chester I. Barnard, *The Functions of the Executive* (Cambridge, Mass.: Harvard University Press, 1960).

4. Richard M. Cyert and James March, *A Behavioral Theory of the Firm* (Englewood Cliffs, N.J.: Prentice-Hall, 1967).

5. Ibid., p. 102.

6. Ibid., pp. 101–02.

7. David Silverman, *The Theory of Organizations: A Sociological Framework* (New York: Basic Books, 1971).

8. Ibid., pp. 3–4.

9. Phillip Selznick, *Leadership in Administration* (New York: Harper & Row, 1957).

10. Alfred D. Chandler, Jr., *Strategy and Structure* (Cambridge, Mass.: The MIT Press, 1962).

11. Max Weber, *The Theory of Social and Economic Organization* (New York: The Free Press, 1964).

12. Karl Popper, *Objective Knowledge* (Oxford: The Clarendon Press, 1972).

13. Edwin Archibald Murray, "The Implementation of Social Policies in Commercial Banks," D.B.A. dissertation, Graduate School of Business, Harvard University, 1974.

14. W. Ross Ashby, *Design for a Brain* (London: Chapman & Hall and Science Paperbacks, 2nd edition, 1972), p. 81.

15. Ibid.

16. Ibid., p. 83.

17. Aaron Wildavsky, *The Politics of the Budgetary Process* (Boston: Little, Brown, 1964; Second edition, 1974).

18. Ibid., second edition.

19. Ibid., pp. xii–xiii.

20. Emery and Trist, "Casual Texture of Organizational Environments."

21. James D. Thompson, *Organizations in Action* (New York: McGraw-Hill, 1967).

1/
TOWARD THE SYSTEMATIC MANAGEMENT OF ORGANIZATIONS:

A HISTORICAL PERSPECTIVE ON MANAGEMENT

The development of management thought is anything but ancient history. The difficulties faced by the organizers of the first large-scale, complex organizations are essentially similar to those faced by managers today. For the first time in history, the early organizers were confronted by problems that were overwhelmingly matters of coordination, control, and oganization. These were administrative or managerial problems, not technical problems. The frameworks evolved by the early theorists were intended to systematically incorporate into the organization the methods (not merely the reiterated details) of earlier successful practice. Thus they sought to institutionalize earlier learning, and insure the replication of successful practice. These responses form a model for the development of a theory of organizational learning, and the basis for extension of this theory in later chapters.

1/

TWO THINKERS:
TAYLOR AND CHURCH

American industry grew and developed tremendously in the decades immediately preceding the turn of the Twentieth Century. For the first time in history, the problems of managing large-scale enterprises appeared widely as industrial organizations began to replace individual entrepreneurs and partnerships as the usual form of operation. The problems were many: increasing complexity and division of labor required more managers, and more coordination among them. Growing trends to specialization and high volume production exacerbated the difficulties. The task quickly burgeoned beyond the capacity of any single individual, however gifted. The problems were those of management, not of production technology. The solutions which evolved, and the theoretical viewpoints developed, provide useful models for exploring present-day dilemmas.

The development of management thought has been marked by two main trends. The first is an attempt to rise above the concrete details of the task to think about what is being done, rather than merely to do it. Until this logical shift is made, coordination, forecasting, and real control are impossible. If management was ever to go beyond a purely reactive stance, mired in details and forever fire-fighting, the shift was essential.

The second trend visible in the development of management is a continuing attempt to transcend dependence upon the skills, memory, or capacity of any single individual. By recording the specifics of a task, a given outcome could be replicated by others: it could be built into a formal system, institutionalized and independent of the individual. Instead of depending on each individual to discover anew the steps to be carried out, instructions could be specified. In this way too, greater predictability could be achieved for given portions of the task, making possible further developments in coordination and control of the task as a whole. Thus the two trends of *thinking about* and *systematizing*, or recording to insure replicability, are interrelated.

5

These developments constituted a thoroughgoing revolution in management practice, nowhere more visible than in the metal-working industry during the last 15 years or so of the Nineteenth Century, where it first took place. A new means of impounding knowledge, independent of the individual's memory—a new technology of management—grew from the strains of continued growth and the increasing subdivision of labor.

THE METAL-WORKING INDUSTRY, 1885–1900

American management of 1885–1900* was beset by a paradox. On the one hand, the management literature of the era extolled the virtues of American practice, buttressing the argument with economic fact: American-made goods competed favorably in European markets despite substantially higher U.S. wages and the added burden of transatlantic shipping rates.[1] However, the very same journals that documented these advantages—most notably the *Transactions of the American Society of Mechanical Engineers, American Machinist,* and *Engineering Magazine*—lamented the chaotic disorganization of U.S. industry as well.

The paradox was to be found in an extreme form in the metal-working industry.† The problem was one of "hard" technological advancement unmatched (in 1885, at least) by comparable advances in the technology‡ of management. Metal working benefited from the application of power to a far greater extent than textiles. Whereas a flying shuttle, powered by hand, is almost as fast as a power loom, a metal lathe or drill under power produces several times the output of a hand-powered tool. Simply because metal is so hard, relative to textiles, wood, or leather, power makes a bigger

---

*I have relied heavily in this section on an article by Joseph A. Litterer, "Systematic Management: The Search for Order and Integration," *Business History Review*, 35 (Winter 1961). For the first portion of this chapter especially, my obligation will be apparent to anyone familiar with Prof. Litterer's work, cited hereafter as "Order and Integration." In addition, my thinking was shaped by the work of Alfred D. Chandler, Jr. See especially his *The Visible Hand: The Managerial Revolution in American Business* (Cambridge: Harvard University Press, 1977).

†Although, as Litterer notes, the developments, problems, and solutions were by no means limited to metal working industries, or indeed to manufacture. Littterer, "Systematic Management: Design for Organizational Recoupling in American Manufacturing Firms," *Business History Review*, 37 (Winter 1963), pp. 369–91; p. 371. (Cited hereafter as "Design for Recoupling.")

‡"Technology" is used here in its widest sense, as "knowledge of how to do something," rather than being limited to machinery, to scientific knowledge, or to production techniques. Specifically, programs and protocols are included here, following Litterer, *Analysis of Organizations* (New York: Wiley, 2nd ed. 1973). This expanded definition is particularly appropriate for discussing management, and "management technology."

difference in working it. There was, therefore, substantial economic incentive to investing in power tools, and U.S. industry did just that. Capital investment, in its turn, and the possibility of greatly expanded throughput, created reinforcing pressures toward specialization. Specialization made special-purpose machinery more feasible; and expensive, specialized machinery paid off only if it was fully utilized. These interactive trends increased throughput even more.

The benefits of specialization were delineated as early as the Eighteenth Century by Adam Smith, who noted that appropriately dividing the job allowed the most expensive, skilled laborers to be reserved to more difficult tasks, where greater strength or skill was required. Easier portions of the job could be carried out by less expensive, less skilled workers. Thus the most difficult segment of the task was no longer the minimum criterion for selection of a laborer.[2]

Charles Babbage, writing *On the Economy of Machinery and Manufactures* in 1832, noted that similar economies could be had in learning time, materials wastage during learning, changeover time in beginning a new task, or in shifting to a different tool, and in the time required to attain a given level of skill through repetition. All of these benefits accrued from the division of labor, and thus encouraged it. Moreover, Babbage remarked, "The division of labor suggests the contrivance of tools and machinery to execute its progress."[3] Thus special-purpose machinery further lessened the cost of labor by performing many tasks hitherto done by hand, or by assisting in difficult tasks. Benefits also grew from increasing subdivision of the work, as workers concentrated on parts of the task.

It was these concepts which were adopted by the American metalworking industry of the late Nineteenth Century, with conspicuous success and in contrast to their European counterparts. The Europeans nurtured a craftsman tradition, in which "a machinist was expected to, could, and did make a simple farm implement or a locomotive and just about every type of metal implement in between."[4] Here in the United States, highly skilled workers were employed only on the more difficult jobs: setting up a semiautomatic machine for a less skilled worker to run, or perhaps making the semiautomatic machine to make the product.[5]

The same hardness of material that made power such a valuable asset in metal working also made increased precision possible.[6] Metal could be worked to closer tolerances than wood or leather. Precision came through specialization, the extensive use of machinery in place of hand labor, and the adoption of special-purpose tools which performed a limited array of tasks with ever-increasing accuracy. Too, simpler tasks could be taught to less skilled workers who nevertheless could achieve acceptable precision within a narrow specialty. Since semi-skilled workers were cheaper, there was economic incentive here, too, to subdivide tasks ever more minutely, and to make them more repetitive.

Interchangeable parts, in such industries as lock-making, clock-making, and so on, are the logical outcome of the economics of specialization, increased throughput, and the possibilities of precision that metal working offered. Metal parts could be precisely made; specialization and special-purpose machinery made more of the parts, precisely; and interchangeable parts made use of the substantially increased throughput. All of this led, at the same time, to lower costs per part and per assembled item. The assembly of standard parts, which did not have to be fitted together by hand by a highly skilled craftsman, became a semi-skilled task. Economics mandated increased volume so that the same return could be had with lower-priced units. Power, specialization, and interchangeable parts (dependent upon increased precision) are all elements setting the stage for the coming of mass production and the problems of coordinating it in the metal-working industry of 1885–1900.

The Need for Integration

To adequately subdivide the multitude of tasks a machinist might be called upon to perform, in order to gain both higher precision and expanded output, manufacturing tasks had to be finely subdivided. First, firms tended to specialize and to subdivide.[7] The sheer process of subdividing the labor to be performed increased the administrative burden enormously. Large shops, with many workers, were divided into many departments, so that diverse and specialized responsibilities—different parts of a single manufacturing task, or ancillary processes such as ordering raw materials, or packaging and shipping the finished product—could be kept track of. Specialization in supervision, as in the performance of a task, made economic sense. As a result, however, since one person could not supervise an unlimited number of workers, levels of hierarchy, as well as divisions within a level, proliferated. This was especially true where much of the knowledge was acquired on the job and remained the possession of the individual, and not codified into procedures and rules. As a result, upper level management became progressively more isolated from knowledge of task performance. Amid the subdivision, no single person could acquire personal expertise in a multitude of specialties. Knowledge, in its specialized details, exploded to simply overwhelming proportions.

The management literature of the time, harkening back to simpler days, still offered normative solutions that must have appeared impossible even to those suggesting them:

> The manager's desk should be the Alpha and Omega of every transaction. It should also be the information bureau of the establishment. No work should be done without the manager's authority and sanction. He should be posted in all things relative to the various stages of the work in operation, and the knowledge should be reliable and easy of access.[8]

In the presence of extensive specialization, no manager was competent to make all the decisions, even if he had the time to do so. Without some systematic reorganizing of the management task, allowing logical abstraction and generalization, the complexity of specialized production brought only the proliferation of detail. Management in "the old slip-shod way of our forefathers"[9] was clearly insufficient. John Tregoing, in one of the very first books on factory operation, summarized the state of management in a descriptive passage which deserves reproduction, despite its length:

> It has been said that "System" is the triumph of "Mind Over Matter," and there is no doubt about the truth herein contained; we only get suspicious of the fact when taking a measured survey of the inner workings of some large factories, and gaze sorrowfully at the triumph of *Matter* Over Mind.
>
> I have heard it remarked that in business three things are necessary: knowledge, temper, and time; but I have seen all three prostrate and powerless for want of *method in management*. Such is the evil of working in an unmethodical and slipshod manner, that it is not too much to say results have followed well-nigh ruinous to the concern.
>
> There is no doubt that the subject of Factory Organization has been sadly neglected in past years. That we have not advanced with the order of the times is the complaint I lodge against the doors of many managers. We are working on old systems which have served their day and generation, systems which "have had their day," but unfortunately have not "ceased to be"; for a brief glance at many of them, both great and small, will prove that little or no method is used, and that the concern moves under conditions which are disgraceful: the wonder is how it moves at all. My observations have led me to conclude . . . that the first and foremost want of many of our large factories is not work, but a thorough revision of the machinery that manages and directs the whole concern. It is not a want of brains; it is not the difficulty of working out a vast and complicated scheme; it is not a matter of involving the company in a large outlay of money—it is simply a question of *method*, the application of a few simple rules, and a respect for the time-honored principle that Order is the First Law of the Universe, and the nearer our approach to it the more harmonious will our arrangements work.[10]

In 1899, J. Slater Lewis noted widespread incidence of the same problem:

> The present is a time of transition . . . old-fashioned methods of administration are beginning to show signs of wearing out and of being no longer equal to the strain and intensity of modern industrial working. Very searching questions are, consequently, frequently asked as to the probable direction in which the reorganization is required.[11]

Taylor's "Scientific Management"

For want of a method, the actual details of operation, minutely sub-divided and beyond the comprehension of management, were left of necessity to the laborers. In 1885, this was so to a degree almost unimaginable today. Because there was, as yet, no codified body of knowledge on "how to do it," as the technology of a production changed, management was farther isolated from the details of operation. As Frederick Taylor noted in 1911,[12] there was a "profound ignorance of employers and their foremen as to the time in which various kinds of work should be done, and this ignorance is shared largely by the workmen." The result was what Taylor called "systematic soldiering": workers marked time on the job, restricting output to a quota. Better methods, increased speeds, properly shaped and adjusted tools, and, most importantly, minutely specified procedures—all lacking when Taylor began—had to be provided to overcome this ignorance and to maximize output. Not incidentally, the concept of such direction being within management's prerogative had also to be established. Until Taylor, the operation of a metal-working shop was dependent upon particular workers, on individuals and their private knowledge of the job. There could be no control where management lacked detailed knowledge about the job. The system or method Taylor proposed rested upon "scientific observation" through time study, and an elaborate records-keeping paraphernalia. The aim was replicability: getting the worker to duplicate what observation had uncovered as "the one best way." To achieve control over throughput, procedures and the precise times in which they were to be carried out had to be specified. So, too, did information flows, to facilitate administrative control. Only thus could management reintegrate diverse, specialized, and highly subdivided tasks into a controlled, predictable whole.

Taylor's approach went beyond the concepts of Babbage and Smith, not only in making specific the abstractions of the earlier writers, but more importantly in moving to prescription of the elemental operations that made up a task. Taylor's concern for minutiae is astounding:

> As an example of these elementary operations which occur in all machine shops, I would cite picking up a bolt and a clamp and putting the bolt head into the slot of a machine, then placing a distance piece under the back end of the clamp and tightening down the bolt. Now this is one of a series of simple operations that take place in every machine shop hundreds of times a day. It is clear that a series of motions such as this can be analyzed, and the best method of making each of these motions can be found out, and then a time study can be made to determine the exact time which a man should take for each job when he

does his work right, without any hurry and yet who does not waste time.*

In theory at least, if the elementary motions could be timed, a composite could be built up. As Taylor himself noted, the result would not be absolute precision, but "a vastly closer approximation as to time than we had ever had before."†

These initial ideas led logically into Taylor's famous metal-cutting experiments. In the 1880s there were no standard speeds or feeds for running power tools. Usually workers made their own tools, and shaped, ground, and sharpened them to suit their individual fancy. In methods as in time, the workers were left to their own devices. Here, too, Taylor became convinced that there was "one best way" to be found. In the course of extended experiments over some 26 years, Taylor and his collaborators discovered that higher speeds produced vastly increased throughput. They discovered that a stream of water, played on the nose of a cutting tool, allowed it to be operated at higher speeds. They found that it was more economical to use the highest grade steel for *all* cutting tools (rather than saving it for difficult jobs) because the increased output more than covered the difference in tool-steel costs. They also discovered the best way to grind particular tools, and the best angles at which a tool should be held against the work.

Yet the technical knowledge alone was not enough. A means for implementing it, for monitoring the worker's practice, and for assuring that new jobs were timed and properly specified had also to be built. To carry all these discoveries into practice, Taylor instituted a central tool room, from which standard cutting tools were checked out, properly prepared and sharpened to a standard rule, suitable for the job at hand and specified by work rules. He constructed a new shop at Midvale (where he worked and carried out many of the early experiments) to get water to the cutting machines. And he constructed an elaborate system of time studies,

---

*Taylor's testimony before the Special House Committee to Investigate the Taylor and other Systems of Shop Management under Authority of House Resolution 90, Washington, D.C.: U.S. Government Printing Office, 1912. Cited in F.B. Copley, *Frederick Taylor: Father of Scientific Management* (New York and London: Harper and Brothers, 1923), I, p. 223. Copley is the standard biographer of Taylor.

†Copley, I, 235. Taylor's accomplishment in specifying what the actions and their times *should* be is an important step beyond Charles Babbage's use of a watch in recording the operatons and times necessary in the manufacture of pins. Taylor's approach was "analytic" and "constructive," rather than merely descriptive, as was Babbage's. Taylor's aim was to prescribe specific movements and times. See Wren, pp. 117–18 for a comparison of Taylor's time-study with the work of Babbage.

records, and instructions. He aimed at recording all relevant information so that the business enterprise was no longer dependent upon individual expertise. Instead, if the details were noted minutely enough, the job could be taught to a less-skilled worker, rather than employing a more expensive, higher-skilled worker to discover it anew. By specifying the details, management could insure the replication of the best practice. As an example of the level of detail, here is Taylor's method of assuring that machines were properly oiled:

> Lists were made out of all the oil holes and surfaces to be oiled; these stating to what part of the machines the holes conducted the oil, and the kind of oil to be used in each case. Duplicates of these lists were filed in the office; and here we can see an early development of the principle of reducing all recurrent procedure to standard practice and recording it. The ordinary way is to leave such procedure entirely to some individual, who in the course of time may work out a pretty good method. All of this knowledge, however, he carries in his head; so that if he falls ill, the procedure suffers, and if he quits the business, someone else must work it out all over again.[13]

It is notable here that Taylor institutionalized the savings in "learning time" that Babbage mentioned, by eliminating the necessity for rediscovery of the best way. Copley continues:

> Taylor not only required the management to determine *right at the start* the best method, but by his records he made the business independent of the comings and goings of individuals, and his records served as insurance against mistakes, failures of memory, and human fallibility in general.[14]

The details of such minute and specific procedure had to be organized, however, if they were to be accessibly retained. Thus an elaborate standing order file, a tickler system for calling things to attention, and a number of clerks to perform various record-keeping tasks, instructions, and so on, were needed. These constitute the core of an administrative staff, the organizational superstructure required by Taylor's separation of task planning and specification from task implementation. It was the planning, subdividing, coordinating, and the discovery of the "one best way"—no less than instruction in it, and enforcement of this criterion of performance—that Taylor saw as the "inconceivable" work of managing scientifically which management must take upon itself as its portion of the bargain with the worker. The benefits were substantial, in metal working. Using harder tool-steel alone gave a five-fold advantage over the old practice. But the details must be seen, too, to insure that the one best way was taken. "If there are no rules, there can be no exceptions,"[15] and management would be back to the old dependence on individuals.

Clearly the elaborate structure of supervision and specification that Taylor proposed (with its attendant precision of detail, its minutiae, and its records) could scarcely be justified where the task at hand was not repetitive. It is only when the cost of the supervisory apparatus can be amortized across many units that the sizable initial expense can be justified. The details and their investigation and recording constitute a capital investment, just as does machinery for special purposes. Similarly, too, if production volume is not maintained, the administrative structure, like the precision possibilities inherent in hard materials, special tools, interchangeable parts, and semi-skilled labor doing clearly specified, limited and repetitive tasks also pushes toward increased throughput. Everything tends toward a higher volume of identical pieces. And, like the other elements, administrative detail itself is encouraged by high-volume production. High volume can be dealt with by staff departments—and staff departments demand high volume to support their expense.

The proliferation of administrative tasks made a differentiation between line and staff imperative. Thus Taylor's split between planning and performance is realized not only in the planning versus the performance of the task, but also in the management of it.* This specialization of the management function has important implications. Duties are subdivided and the focus narrowed, just as in the actual performance of the work. All of the advantages noted by Babbage and Smith for the division of the performance of labor would seem to apply as well to the management of that performance. Thus the time required to learn a managerial job and the potential for error are reduced, and the level of skill in performing the task is acquired with more frequent repetitions of a smaller segment of the managerial task as a whole. Importantly, the level of skill demanded of the manager decreases as well.

Taylor listed the nine qualities of a "well-rounded" foreman:

Brains,
Education,
Special or technical knowledge, manual dexterity or strength,
Tact
Energy,

---

*Litterer. "Design for Recoupling," p. 387, notes the evidence of existence of staff, differentiated from line in their tasks, well before Harrington Emerson's theoretical argument for staff.

FIGURE 1.1

Taylor's "Functional Foremen"

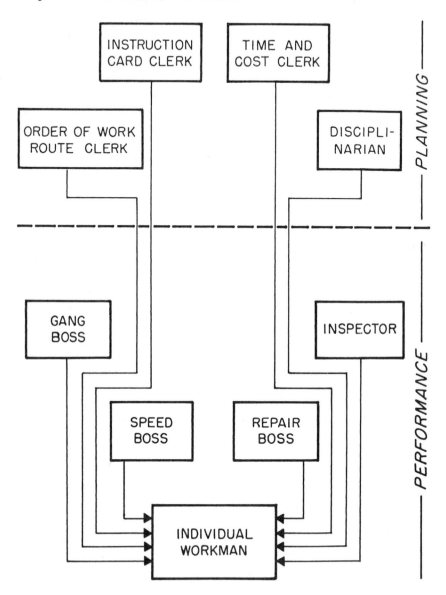

Source: Adapted from F.B. and L.M. Gilbreth, *Applied Motion Study* (New York: Sturgis and Walton Co., 1917).

Grit,
Honesty,
Judgment or common sense, and
Good health.

As Taylor noted, finding a candidate with three of these traits was not difficult. Those with four traits were "higher priced." Finding a candidate who possessed five of these traits began to be difficult, while those who possessed six, seven, or eight were "almost impossible to get."[16]

The more specific skills required to manage the manufacturing processes which were Taylor's concern are reduced by the same logic, however. The performance managers—gang boss, speed boss, repair boss, and inspector—have no need of the specialized clerical skills essential to the planning managers' jobs. Similarly, the planning staff—order of work route clerk, instruction clerk, time and cost clerk, and disciplinarian—have no need of the level of technical expertise required for the performance managers' jobs. Taylor's "functional management" is an important application of the idea of subdivision of labor to management. As such, it simplifies and reduces the overwhelming and yet critical task of managing the technical detail of a large, complex organization with extensively subdivided labor.

Subdivision of the labor of management facilitates the acquisition of knowledge in the individual manager by limiting the scope of a given managerial job. The apparatus of the planning department (instruction cards, time study, and so on) insure that the knowledge, once acquired, is not limited to the manager presently in the job, but instead is accessible to anyone who can read. Thus in management, as in the performance of a task, Taylor's system moved the organization toward independence of individuals, and towards an increased control, through specifying required behaviors.

Finally, subdivision of the managerial task and institutionalization of routine details also reduced the scope of the general managerial job. By establishing a routine and the mechanisms for monitoring it, Taylor's system effectively eliminated the need for a general manager to concern himelf with the details. These were delegated and decentralized. The scarce and valuable resource of top-level management skills could thereby be reserved for the exceptions. Here, too, it is clear that Taylor's approach implied a sophisticated extension of the concept of division of labor applied to managerial work. It was left to others to make this extension explicit, however, and to develop the more general framework of theory in which it could make sense. Among the thinkers responsible for the extension was Alexander Hamilton Church, to whom I shall turn next.

Alexander Hamilton Church

Another early management thinker was Alexander Hamilton Church.* Although far less well-known than his contemporary, Church developed ideas more fundamental and inclusive than those of Taylor. In his concern for coordination and in his explicit consideration of the specialization of the managerial function, Church might be said to begin where Taylor leaves off. Church's contributions fall into two main areas: cost accounting and general management theory. Each area is essential: without the general theory, there is no framework within which to coordinate. Without the accounting techniques, coordination cannot be achieved, for the necessary details are simply overwhelming. Church contributed substantially to the development of unified control systems, which made possible the efficient flow of information about operations that enabled managers to control their organizations. Without the kinds of control systems described by Church, control in a complex organization with line and staff divisions, even in so rudimentary a form as Taylor's "functional foremen," is impossible as soon as the planning staff deals with more than one product or area.

Church noted the fundamental importance of coordination going well beyond the kind of technical concentration that was Taylor's forte:

> Reform begins and generally ends with the modernizing of machinery and nonproductive appliances in that department, such as cranes, shop-transport, tool-rooms and the like, leaving untouched the system of nerves, by which the whole is directed. . . . The general effect of leaving this important section out of account is much the same as that of trying to restore life to a dying man by mounting him on a bicycle, instead of by building up the decaying tissue first.
>
> Small wonder it is that drastic reorganization often fails to give relief. Coordination is the keynote of modern industry, but it is a work of which the meaning is too often ignored by would-be reformers.[17]

In Church's view, the underlying need for coordination rested upon the limitations of the human mind, faced with the exploding complexity of specialization, detail and rapid technical development:

> The necessity for coordination . . . is an inevitable result of the evolution of the factory, no one mind can grasp and hold all the details.

------

*In the following discussion, I have drawn heavily upon an excellent article by Joseph A. Litterer, "Alexander Hamilton Church and the Development of Modern Management," *Businss History Review* 35 (Summer 1961), pp. 211–25, as well as upon Church's own works.

> The object of modern administrative organization is to readjust the balance of responsibilities disturbed by the expansion of industrial operations, and to enable the central control to be restored in its essential features.[18]

By restoring control "in its essential features," however, Church clearly meant something more than controlling minute detail—focusing not on the details, but on how they fit together.

Church saw the proliferation of information and detail as explicitly and specifically extending to management, thereby requiring specialization and the division of managerial labor, even as the work of production was subdivided. From the most inclusive and abstract viewpoint, the two functions of management, distinct but interrelated, were the *Determinative* and the *Administrative*. Church's Determinative function is what we would term the policy formulation aspect of general management. The Administrative function, to which Church confines his attentions, "takes the policy as determined, and gives it practical expression in buying, making, and selling."[19] These definitions are logically far more inclusive than concentration on the efficiency of the individual worker (although clearly the Administrative function would be concerned with that as well). Church draws the distinction between his work and Taylor's in very much these terms. First, he notes that "the five great organic functions" into which he divides all managerial work "have no relation to what is termed 'functional foremanship'."[20] Next, he argues that there is an explicit distinction between technical and administrative knowledge—an insight made use of in later chapters.

> The technical efficiency of operations is not part of the science of administration. The action of dyes, the strength of yarns, the properties of materials, the strength of castings, the wearing properties of silk ties, the durability of steel rails, are not in the province of an administration expert, but in that of a *technical* expert in one or other of the industries concerned. In other words, the technical basis of operations is not a part of the science of management.[21]

This is so even though technical expertise and the proper relationship between technical processes is essential. The distinction between technical and administrative knowledge is of utmost importance. Where technical knowledge is *content*, administrative knowledge concerns the *coordination and control* of the content—the overall fitting together of functions. Said another way, administrative knowledge is "about" how to use use technical knowledge.

Church identified two distinct types of management techniques, analysis and synthesis:

> The main distinction between synthesis and analysis in this connection is that synthesis is concerned with fashioning means to effect large ends, and analysis is concerned with the correct local use of given means. . . . The view taken by analysis . . . is a narrow and limited one; it concerns itself with the infinitely small. Its task is to say "how to use certain means to the best advantage." . . . But the synthetical side of management demands that every effort of analysis, like every other effort made in the plant, shall have some proportion, some definite economic relation to the purpose for which the business is being run.[22]

In insisting upon the importance of synthesis, Church emphasized organizing and coordinating the activities of the enterprise as a whole. Analytical tools—like time and motion studies, remuneration schemes, and the like—were merely means to assist in the larger process. Synthesis and analysis were complementary, rather than antagonistic. But since all activities carried on in a business were best seen in functional terms, synthetic thinking was critical:

> To paraphrase a famous saying, we may assert that "men may come and men may go, but the function goes on forever." It is evident therefore that the study of functions is of the greatest importance. But those functions are a product of synthesis—analysis would never organize them nor coordinate them.[23]

From another perspective, we may describe Church's "synthetic thinking" as rising up a level of logical abstraction to construct a pattern from what is observed. Conversely, analytic thinking descends a logical level to concrete specifics.

Church identified five inclusive and mutually exclusive organic functional areas in production:

> No form of activity exists in a manufacturing plant *for the purposes of production* that does not come under one or other of these functional divisions. Consequently, we can say that production is a synthesis of Design, Equipment, Control, Comparison, and Operation.[24]

By Design, Church meant design of the product—"prescribing in advance the changes which shall successively take place in material."[25] Equipment included procurement of the equipment, its maintenance, repairs, replacement, and efficient layout. Layout, incidentally, in terms of flow of materials, machine placement, and so on, evolves directly from a concern for overall coordination as distinct from the suboptimizing tendency apparent in Taylor's focus on the efficient actions of the individual. Control is keeping track of the passage of materials through the production process, start to finish. It includes keeping track of both process and work in progress, and also providing proper coordination of instructions and materials, "so that one does not have to wait for another."[26] In observing that this is particularly true in the metal-working industry, where charts, drawings, and instructions are frequently as essential to the proper performance of work as the raw materials themselves, Church is following Taylor. In his concern for coordinating instruction with materials, however, Church transcends Taylor. Church's categories are not limited to the metal-working industry (nor were Taylor's). As Church noted, coordination of this kind is present, if more rudimentary, in all industries.

Comparison, Church's fourth function, matches actual behavior, process, or output to a standard, whether in physical goods, workers' tasks, cost or time. Here again, Taylor led the way in prescribing a standard; Church generalized the notion to a principle far beyond shop management. Comparison rests upon observation and record, and upon some metric which permits evaluation. Operation, the final function, includes the actual workings of the shops. However, it includes only that work directly upon the materials being transformed. It explicitly does not include supervision, which is a part of Control, or inspection, which is a part of Comparison.[27]

Church's categories distinguish between technical and administrative knowledge, and between the analytical nature of the underlying portions and the synthetic nature of the overall management task, which is coordination. The distinction is clearly between the particular and the general, as well:

> In every industry, and even in most plants in the same industry, the department of Operation *is* peculiar and individual. But in every industry the functions and principles of administration are universally applicable, and a large number of their variables are common to a wide range of industries, to say nothing of plants.[28]

Church saw these distinctions as a way of specializing the labor of management, of focusing attention clearly on whatever area required it, while holding others constant. Since each function has its own problems, they must be resolved within that function. Nevertheless, hindrances—such as irregularities in the supply of power—may cause problems from outside a function. Church's point is that the absence of these hindrances does not in and of itself insure efficient performance *within* a function. Thus even in th absence of irregularities in the power supply, the function of Operation may not be efficient.

Church's observations on overhead expenses and ancillary tasks form the second major facet of his contribution to the development of administrative systems for systematically managing organizations. Given the notion of specialized managerial labor, planning and coordinating functions, and so on, some means of accounting for these indirect expenses and of measuring their impact was essential. Church provided this, in his treatment of overhead.

Unlike others of his time, who saw overhead as "unnecessary" expense to be reduced or eliminated where possible, Church saw clearly that such expenditures were legitimate adjuncts to actual operation: "Every legitimate expense in a machine shop is incurred for the purpose of getting the work up to, under, or away from the tool point, in one way or another."[29] Subsidiary activities, however complex and numerous, are to be assessed as they contribute to this end. By subsidiary activities, Church went far beyond the machine-operator's wages, which he considered obvious and straightforward. The remaining 100 to 200 percent of direct operative labor, "usually jumbled together into a common fund termed expense burden"[30] and estimated at some proportion of direct labor, must be analyzed to ascertain the operation cost per hour of each machine.

This aim evolves out of the view of production as the synthesis of organic functions. These functions or activities are the basis of analysis, and constitute the activities of which production is only one: "*Actual production is the last organization* [organized and coordinated set of activities] *in a chain of related but separate* organizations."[31] All of the non-manufacturing activities required to manufacture economically and efficiently are legitimately chargeable as "machine rent." Expense burden, the cost of these ancillary activities, is not a cost of production, but a cost of capacity to produce.[32] The various costs of ancillary activities are, says Church, to be kept track of separately from one another, and measured appropriately—not lumped under the common measure of direct labor percentages as was the general practice. Thus the cost for power is best measured in terms of horsepower consumed, and shop rental is more meaningfully defined in terms of rate per square foot than as a percentage of labor. In this way, "The exact bearing of that particular non-manufacturing function called property-owning on capacity to produce is ascertained. . . ."[33]

Church's method permits the calculation of the cost of property ownership in terms that allow it to be compared with rental. Thus alternatives fall within a logical scheme which relates them all to the capacity to produce. Church's method also allows a more rational treatment of capacity utilization. By this method, production cost is not affected by conditions in the shop: "You must not punish the job because part of your capacity to produce is being wasted."[34] Further, the proportion of capacity utilization is now discernible, making possible more rational decisions when expanded output is required. It is senseless to add productive capacity when operating efficiency is the bottleneck; Church's method makes it possible to perceive this condition.

Church's final contribution is again theoretical. In the *American Machinist* in 1912, Church and Leon Pratt Alford published their "Principles of Management,"[35] providing an inclusive framework within which they place both Taylor and other earlier thinkers. "The basic regulative principles of management" are three: the systematic use of experience; the economic control of effort; and the promotion of personal effectiveness. Church and Alford's "systematic use of experience" is a concept fundamental to notions of organizational learning. Like Taylor, Church and Alford clearly have more in mind than mere repetition of what has always been done. Many of Taylor's concepts, and many extensions of them, are included:

> Experience is the knowledge of past attainment. It includes a knowledge of *what* has been done, and also *how* it has been done. It is inseparably associated with standards of performance, that is with the ideas of quantity and quality in relation to any particular method of doing something.
>
> The great instrument of experience, which makes progress possible, is "comparison." By systematic use of experience is meant the careful analysis of what is about to be attempted, and its reference to existing records and standards of performance.[36]

Systematic observations and their recording, prescribed actions and methods, and carefully selected experimental observations to fill in gaps in present knowledge are all part of the principle Church and Alford espouse. They have obviously sought to go far beyond Taylor in generality, however. The principles are equally applicable to routine and to new situations, particularly where analytic thinking may be used—much as Taylor himself advocated the use of elemental actions to build a sequential estimate of a new job, or as Galbraith sought "therbligs." Further still, the principles enunciated by Church and Alford are applicable at higher levels of logic—they are not limited to the concrete details of oiling a machine, laying bricks, or even constructing a time-keeping system. They are applicable to systems of management as well. Thus "systematic use of experience" impounds most of Taylor's "Scientific Management," and most of Emerson's "Twelve Principles." Church and Alford sought generality—and with proper definition, their notion of "systematic use of experience" can be carried far toward a definition of organizational learning. This theme will be dealt with at length in a later chapter.

In summary, then, Church's contributions to management thought are more extensive than his anonymity would suggest. His viewpoint of the funtion of management—as inclusive and coordinative, rather than merely technical or concrete—is central to management theory down to the present. Church's contributions also include, in the same global and (in his words) "synthetic" fashion, the view that all non-manufacturing functions are to be evaluated for their contribution to the central production process. The idea predates the jargon of analysis of organizational throughput by many years. The system of cost accounting which Church developed, consonant with this thinking, was designed to permit the appropriate evaluation of subsidiary processes. These concepts, too, remain in use today.

THE CONTRIBUTION OF TAYLOR AND CHURCH AND SYSTEMATIC MANAGEMENT

Systematic management, then, bequeathed an ideal, a pattern of thought, and a number of important management tools. The ideal was that of the enterprise as a unified whole, controlled and coordinated in a systematic, rational fashion. In the light of the chaotic state of factory practice when these thinkers began—as reported in the journals and articles cited at length in this chapter—envisioning the ideal was no mean accomplishment. The ideal provided an important guide. The pattern of thought was the beginning of what we call management: the framework of the overall aim or purpose of the endeavor, and the notion of coordinating all activities toward that single end. While both the ideal and the pattern of thought seem obvious today, they were not clear between 1880 and 1912. Of necessity, the developing pattern of thought was increasingly comprehensive, capable of subsuming and transcending the concrete details of the activities it was intended to order. To say this in another fashion, the pattern of thought was *about* the activities it ordered; it was a logical system up one level from those activities. The means for including the concrete details within the larger managerial framework were the administrative systems and managerial tools developed by the Systematic Management thinkers, most notably Taylor and Church.* The tools ranged from production control, inventory control, and cost-accounting systems (frequently treated as three aspects of a single administrative system of control in the literature of the period) to the concept of management by exception first advocated by Taylor to the techniques of time and motion studies.

_____

*Clearly the list could be expanded substantially; in the field of accounting systems alone, Church must stand for a company that includes J. Slater Lewis, whose student Church was; Capt. Henry Metcalfe, whose *Cost of Manufacturers and the Administration of Workshops, Public and Private* stated the proposition that there was a generally applicable "science of administration" and proposed a system for cost and material control in 1885; Hugo Diemer, who wrote on "The Functions and Organization of the Purchasing Department" in

NOTES

1. "The Low Wages 'Boom'," *American Machinist*, Vol. 2 (Aug. 30, 1879), p. 8; J. Schoenhof, *The Economy of High Wages* (New York: G.P. Putnam's Sons, 1893), pp. 22–25, 116–21.

2. Adam Smith. *An Inquiry into the Nature and Causes of the Wealth of Nations* (London: W. Strahen and T. Cadell, 1776). Frequently reprinted.

3. Charles Babbage. "On the Division of Labour," reprinted from *On the Economy of Machinery and Manufactures* (Philadelphia: Carey & Lea, 1832) in: *Classics in Management*, ed. Harwood F. Merrill (American Management Association, n.p., 1970). Babbage is also cited at length in Daniel A. Wren, *The Evolution of Management Thought* (New York: The Ronald Press, 1972), esp. pp. 71–73.

4. H.F.L. Orcutt, "Machine Shop Management in Europe and America. VI. Comparisons as to Efficiency and Methods," *Engineering Magazine* 17 (June 1899), p. 384. Cited in Joseph A. Litterer, "Systematic Management: The Search for Order and Integration," *Business History Review*, 35 (Winter 1961), p. 464.

5. Litterer, "Order and Integration," pp. 466–67.

6. William Rushing. "Hardiness of Materials as Related to Division of Labor in Manufacturing Industries," *Administrative Science Quarterly* 13 (1968), 229–45.

7. Specialization by product is discussed by Litterer in "Design for Organizational Recoupling," p. 371.

8. H.M. Norris. "A Simple and Effective System of Shop Cost-Keeping," *Engineering Magazine* 16(1898), p. 385. Cited in Litterer, "Order and Integration," p. 470.

9. The phrase is Norris's, in "Shop System," *Iron Age* 54 (Nov. 1, 1894), p. 746. Cited in "Order and Integration," p. 473.

10. John Tregoing. *A Treatise on Factory Management* (Lynn, Mass.: Press of T.P. Nichols, 1891), p. iii. Cited in "Order and Integration," p. 473.

11. "Works Management for the Maximum of Production: Organization as a Factory of Output," Engineering Magazine (1899), p. 59. Cited in "Order and Integration," p. 469.

12. In *Shop Management*, first published in the *Transactions of the American Society of Mechanical Engineers* (New York: Published by the Society. J.J. Little and Co. Press, 1903).

13. F.B. Copley. *Frederick Taylor: Father of Scientific Management* (New York and London: Harper and Brothers, 1923), I, p. 270.

14. Ibid.

15. Taylor, Harvard Lectures. In Copley, I, 302.

16. Taylor, *Shop Management*, p. 96.

17. Alexander Hamilton Church. "The Meaning of Commercial Organization," *Engineering Magazine* 20 (1900), pp. 392–93. Cited in Litterer, "Alexander Hamilton Church,' p. 213.

18. Church. "The Meaning of Commercial Organization," p. 395. In Litterer, p. 213.

19. Alexander Hamilton Church. *The Science and Practice of Management* (New York: The Engineering Magazine Co., 1941), p. 1.

20. Ibid., p. 7n.

21. Ibid., p. 57. Emphasis in the original.

Engineering Magazine 18 (1900), p. 833, setting out rules for economic ordering quantities and taking advantage of cash discounts, as well as advocating the use of specialists to keep track of raw material stocks; and others too numerous to mention. In this paper, Taylor and Church are representatives, rather than the only, or even the best known, of their school.

22. Ibid., pp. 24–25.

23. Ibid., p. 26.

24. Ibid., p. 33.

25. Ibid., pp. 29–30.

26. Ibid., p. 31.

27. Ibid., p. 33.

28. Ibid., p. 57.

29. Alexander Hamilton Church. "Distribution of Expense Burden," *American Machinist* (May 25, 1911), p. 991. Emphasis in the original.

30. Ibid., p. 991.

31. Ibid. Emphasis in original.

32. Ibid., p. 996.

33. Ibid.

34. Ibid.

35. Alexander Hamilton Church and Leon Pratt Alford. "The Principles of Management," *American Machinist* 36 (May 30, 1912), pp. 857–61. Rpt. in *Classics in Management*, pp. 169–89.

36. Ibid., p. 171.

2/

TWO COMPANIES:
DU PONT AND GENERAL MOTORS

SYSTEMATIC IDEAS

Taylor and Church and other systematic approaches to management represent an important shift from the uncontrolled, chaotic practices of their predecessors. Before Taylor, responsibility for the task itself was left to the workers. Taylor's investigations gathered together an immense body of knowledge—about metal cutting, oiling machines, and other tasks— which made it possible for the first time to define a "best way." Taylor's elaborate administrative apparatus of clerks, standing orders, and the many "functional foremen" created the mechanism for implementing the knowledge. Implementing meant not only discovering the knowledge, but specifying it; recording it, so that it was independent of the discoverer; organizing it, so that it could be both taught and related to other knowledge; and creating the means both to teach it systematically and to monitor its reproduction.

Church, as well as others, pointed out that Taylor's attentions were predominantly confined to the tasks of the individual workers on the shop floor. However, much extension might be implicit in the *ideas* of creating a systematic body of knowledge about a task, or a mechanism for implementing it. It was left to Church and others to develop the more comprehensive view of the management function which would allow that expansion to take place. Only then was the overall coordination of many tasks and their management possible.

The shift from the delimited task itself to knowledge about it—a wider context of *why* and *how*, rather than the mere rote repetition of *what*—is a shift in logical level. Knowledge about a task is, of necessity, more inclusive than knowing the specific procedures of the task itself. Thus, Taylor's metal-cutting experiments created a framework of knowledge, and of the relationships among bits of knowledge, that is vastly more powerful and inclusive than the specifics of "Set speed at so many revolutions per minute, and feed at so many inches; use such-and-such a tool, to be applied to the work at this angle." Taylor's ideas of a "science" of cutting metals, and of such knowledge being beyond the comprehension of the workers are poorly articulated perceptions of this hierarchical logic. Since Taylor repeatedly spoke of assisting workers to develop to their highest potential, and indeed, of the dearth of "first class" citizens at all levels, he clearly had something more in mind than a rationale for dismissing the laborer as mentally inferior.

Taylor's statements make more sense if they are interpreted as referring to a higher logical level, and a different focus—a systematized and more inclusive knowledge about the task—rather than simply to the concrete specifics of innumerable tasks, which not even Taylor's functional foremen were expected to master in all their details. This interpretation is doubly useful. In the first place, it makes sense of the exhaustive investigations undertaken by Taylor. These investigations make sense only if one is concerned *about* what is being done, rather than with the doing *per se*. A "theory of metal cutting" must of necessity constitute some more inclusive level of logic than any individual task of metal cutting. What is at issue is beyond mere repetition; instead, efficiency, replicability of prior success in circumstances *not* identical, and control of output were all clearly Taylor's aims. If directions are "Follow orders," then it is not possible to compare sets of orders, to choose among them, or to generate new sets of orders. Only a more inclusive *logical* framework—allowing for multiple sets of orders—permits such comparison. The hierarchy is essentially based upon details, their specification, and the examination or change of those specifications in the light of some complex purpose. Thus, the machinist's task (at the lowest level of a logical hierarchy) is to follow orders. Those orders are produced by a systematic study of what is to be done (a higher *logical* level). A higher level still evaluates whether what is to be done is appropriate to the final task, and so on. Such a hierarchic focus is also consonant with Scientific Management's well-known emphasis on authority and responsibility.

Church concentrated on the higher end of this scale, on fitting various tasks together for the benefit of the firm as a whole. Church saw clearly that the firm itself was the level of concern (or logic) within which, for the first time, the various efficiencies advocated by Taylor could be judged and adjusted. Church provided the viewpoint from which the assumptions (for instance, perform *this* task) can be evaluated. If Taylor and Church's views of Systematic Management grew chiefly from the metal-working industry, where problems of complexity, specialization, and coordination were most acute in the decades around the turn of the century, the next order of sophistication occurred elsewhere.

Two giants of American industry, Du Pont and General Motors, were responsible for the next steps in developing systematic managerial methods which made learning an institutional phenomenon, rather than the sole preserve of an individual. These methods allowed managers to cope with enormously larger and more complex enterprises than hitherto. Complex organizations of this size could be run efficiently *only* if they were run systematically. In addition, new techniques permitted the large firms to respond flexibly to changing situations despite their size, by making the levers of change and of dissemination of knowledge accessible to managers. The histories of Du Pont and GM are inextricably linked by the accidents of investment and corporate friendship that drew Pierre S. du Pont, his methods and managers, from the Du Pont Company into GM. The history given here is necessarily partial and abbreviated, concentrating upon institutionalizing learning and methods for change. Nevertheless, the connections between Du Pont and GM, and the contributions of these companies to the systematic management of organizations in changing environments will be clear.*

DU PONT

Before Consolidation

When Pierre S., T. Coleman, and Alfred I. du Pont purchased their family's business for $12 million in 1902, they purchased a sizable but not enormous concern. The company did not control the explosives industry in the United States, nor was it particularly modern or up-to-date in either its equipment or its management practices. To the contrary, it was decidedly backward, as was the explosives industry as a whole. In 1880, Pierre's father, Lammot du Pont, had started a separate firm, the Repauno Chemical Company, to produce dynamite when the then-head of the parent

---

*The reader is referred to Alfred D. Chandler, Jr.'s excellent works for a comprehensive and detailed appraisal of Du Pont and General Motors. See especially *Pierre S. du Pont and the Making of the Modern Corporation* (with Stephen Salsbury) (New York: Harper and Row, 1971); *Strategy and Structure* (Cambridge, Mass.: The MIT Press, 1962); and *Giant Enterprise: Ford, General Motors and the Automobile Industry* (New York: Harcourt, Brace and World, Inc., 1964). I have drawn extensively on Professor Chandler's insights in this chapter. Chandler and Salsbury will be referenced hereafter as Chandler and Salsbury.

See also two illuminating articles by Ernest Dale, "Du Pont and Systematic Management," *Administrative Science Quarterly* (1967), pp. 25–29, and "Contributions to Administration by Alfred P. Sloan, Jr. and GM," *Administrative Science Quarterly* (1956), pp. 30–62. For the GM story, the first and best reference must, of course, be Sloan's *My Years with General Motors* (New York: Doubleday, 1963).

firm, Colonel Henry du Pont, had refused to approve production of the new explosive in the Du Pont Company mills. Colonel Henry's refusal was based upon the conviction that:

> It is only a matter of time *how soon* a man will lose his life who uses Hercules, Giant, Dualin, Dynamite, Nitroglycerine, Guncotton, Averhard's Patent or any explosive of that nature. They are vastly more dangerous than gunpowder, and no man's life is safe who uses them.[1]

This was in 1871, and, as Lammot's departure in 1880 indicated, Colonel Henry's opinions did not change. In 1902, when the cousins purchased the family firm, Du Pont still did not directly control any dynamite production, although the explosive was becoming increasingly important.

In 1890, Pierre received an engineering degree from M.I.T. and joined the old family firm to work at the Upper Powder Yard. "This is where my father, grandfather, and great-grandfather had entered the Company's employ," he wrote with satisfaction at achieving a childhood dream.[2] But he found the old firm not much improved since his father's time. The laboratories where he was to work were shockingly primitive:

> The laboratory, so-called, was in a deplorable condition. . . . The building was a one-story addition to the Saltpetre Refinery, heavy stone walls and not too adequate windows. Equipment was almost nothing. A common kitchen range and one small spirit lamp were the only means of heating for chemical work. No gas or electrical facilities, and a common kitchen sink, and one ordinary three-quarter-inch tap for the water supply. Distilled water came from a supply prepared for use in the refinery; the workmen called it "still-water" which referred more to its escape from ill-treatment more or less in original condition than to any attained purity. Any unusual impurity was accounted for by the words, "she must have boiled over." The laboratory contained no chemical reagents for making ordinary tests and the chemical apparatus was equally deficient in quantity or selection. The chemical balance did not deign to respond to the added weight of a few milligrams, but as it was customary to select the weights by hand without use of forceps, the rough operation of weighing powder samples for drying was sufficiently well accomplished.[3]

Pierre struggled to improve laboratory conditions and get some serious attention paid to new chemical techniques, but the company was slow to respond. "Pierre could make no significant changes," according to Chandler and Salsbury, "not even in the backward chemical laboratory."[4] A transfer in 1899 to the company's new experimental plant for smokeless powder at Carney's Point proved a small enough advance. At one point a cold-snap all but stopped work because ice built up over the floors to a thickness of one to two inches—the laboratory was unheated! As Pierre commented, "It is all the same old trouble of not looking ahead and making provisions for things that are bound to occur sooner or later."[5]

At about this time, Pierre received a very attractive offer from the Johnson Company (where Coleman was employed) of which he was a major stockholder. The offer promised Pierre a chance to exercise his abilities in ways clearly impossible in the family firm. When the senior Du Pont partners declined to arrange a partnership for him, or an executive position in which he might have some effect on management practices in the family firm, he accepted the Johnson Company's offer. As Chandler and Salsbury note:

> Pierre may have left Wilmington with bitterness toward Francis G. du Pont, but his main reason was an inner frustration born of a realization that as long as the old partnership dominated the company there was no possibility that his voice would be heard. Nearly ten years on the Brandywine had sapped his youthful dreams of remaking the company . . . Pierre left with no illusions. He thought his break with Delaware permanent and that his future lay in the West.[6]

New Ownership at Du Pont

Pierre's renewed association with the family firm came dramatically. With the death of Eugene du Pont, the surviving partners found themselves leaderless. Four of them were too old or too ill to assume control of the firm; the fifth, Alfred I. du Pont, was inexperienced and temperamental. The older partners agreed to sell the firm to Laflin & Rand, a long-time, friendly rival firm. To their surprise, rather than see the firm go to outsiders, Alfred proposed to buy it himself, with his cousins Coleman and Pierre. A price of $12 million was quickly agreed upon. As Alfred had neither interest nor experience in administration or finance, he left these tasks to Coleman and Pierre, while he continued to supervise the company's black powder mills. At the time of the purchase, the records and financial controls of the old firm were so lacking that Pierre could write to his brother Irenee:

> I think there is to be some tall hustling to get everything reorganized. We have not the slightest idea of what we are buying, but in that we are probably not at a disadvantage, as I think the old company has a very slim idea of the property they possess.[7]

The cousins' initial intuitions that the firm was undervalued were quickly corroborated. Over a million dollars of the company's assets were in cash and a certified public accountant's valuation revised the initial figure of $12 million upwards to $14,397,924.

The primary difference was in the valuation placed on stock in other companies held by the Du Pont Company. Thus, the potential of the company was certainly undervalued at $12 million. The stocks held by Du Pont were the key to an ambitious strategy of consolidation which Pierre and Coleman soon saw as essential. The Du Pont Company itself operated only a few black powder mills and the new smokeless powder works at Carney's Point; it did not operate a single dynamite works. The stock it held in other firms, including the Repauno Chemical Company started by Pierre's father, extended the Du Pont control. Through the Gunpowder Trade Association, in which voting strength was determined by size, the company controlled much of the industry through stock holdings. After the depression of 1870, Colonel Henry du Pont had purchased controlling interest in more than half-a-dozen of the larger powder companies. These votes represented a majority in the Trade Association. However, the Association exercised no administrative control beyond allotment of production quotas, and price setting:

> Neither the individual companies nor the Association paid much attention to costs, to improving processes, or to developing more systematic purchasing and marketing techniques. There was little coordination between the marketing and selling companies. With only a few notable exceptions, the manufacturing firms sold through agents who handled the output of many companies and who apparently also became members of the Association. Effective administration was impossible because neither the separate firms nor the combination itself had the information or methods to assure an efficient use of existing resources, and so to reduce unit costs and increase output per worker. They did not even have a systematic way of gauging existing or potential demand on which to base their price and production schedules.[8]

Yet to realize the potential of their newly acquired properties, Pierre and Coleman recognized that they must coordinate and manage them as a unified whole. They saw the potential for profit not in continuing as before, but in expanding production while increasing productivity. Economies of scale and efficiencies in production and administration were the means to their end. They wanted a fairly large, full-line company, centrally managed for efficient production and control by the latest methods. These, in turn, could be achieved only by first consolidating the piecemeal stock ownership Du Pont already had in many small companies into a single, centrally administered entity. Control through management, and ownership, rather than through production quotas and price setting, was essential. As Pierre later wrote:

> At the time we made the purchase of the properties, we realized that if a good investment was to be made for us, it would necessitate a complete reorganization of the method of doing business; that the administrative end would have to be reorganized, numerous selling organizations, or

administrative organizations done away with, and we would have to establish a system of costs in order that an economical manufacture could be installed throughout the business. That was prevented, absolutely, by our lack of control of the properties in which we were interested, and we had no means of establishing a new system of organization in any of these companies.[9]

Only by operating the properties in concert, through one set of managers, was it possible to eliminate costly duplication and inefficiency; to achieve effective supervision of production and purchasing, shipping and selling; and to coordinate the functions properly.

To achieve their goal of efficient, centralized administration, Pierre and Coleman reorganized the existing company along functional lines. They integrated a wholly-owned subsidiary, Hazard, into the administrative structure. It was also important to absorb other subsidiaries, particularly those making dynamite. Without this step, the Du Pont Company would not directly operate any dynamite works, and thus would not itself be a full-line company—a serious disadvantage, with dynamite becoming increasingly important. In addition, Du Pont's smokeless powder capacity was expanded by purchase of a competitor. When the plan was accomplished, the company was able to offer a full line of products produced at sufficient volume to attain economies of scale.

It became increasingly clear that all of these goals depended upon Du Pont's control of Laflin & Rand, the friendly rival to whom the older partners had been prepared to offer the family firm. Stock held in other companies was again the key. While Du Pont itself controlled only two black powder companies besides its subsidiary, Hazard, purchase of Laflin & Rand would give it over 50 percent of the stock of 17 companies, and a substantial minority interest in 12 more. This would represent control, or at least a voice in the management, of approximately two-thirds of the black powder production in the eastern United States. In dynamite, as yet, Du Pont did not directly operate any plants. Laflin & Rand stock ownership would give Du Pont a majority holding (and thus control) of Eastern Dynamite, a holding company which controlled almost 70 percent of the dynamite production east of the Rockies. This control was especially important because dynamite was rapidly replacing black powder as the standard blasting explosive. The cousins decided to buy.

Management Information

An inspection of the Laflin & Rand books was even more electrifying than the inspection of the old Du Pont Company's books had been. Numerous items were carried at cost, rather than at anything resembling a market evaluation, substantially understating the value of the firm. This was particularly true for stocks in other companies held by Laflin & Rand. The firm held far more stock than Pierre and Coleman had anticipated, and this was valued even below the very conservative figures carried on the old Du Pont Company's books. Some 5,807 shares of Eastern Dynamite were valued at approximately $31 per share, for instance, while the Du Pont books had noted them at $140, a figure Pierre and Coleman had considered conservative. (See Table 2.1 for the Laflin & Rand Treasurer's statement of June 30, 1902, and Pierre's re-evaluation.)

The sale was quickly consummated, and the new Du Pont Company became a full-line company directly involved in the production of black powder, smokeless powder, and dynamite. They also controlled about two-thirds of the U.S. production of these explosives east of the Rockies. The new company owned outright eight black powder mills formerly held by Laflin & Rand, in addition to plants formerly owned by Du Pont and operating control acquired through majority stock ownership. The total was 21 black powder works, eight dynamite plants, and two smokeless powder facilities.

The great task of reorganization facing the cousins was much akin to those faced by their predecessors, Taylor and Church. Like Taylor, the cousins operated in an industry without a history of systematic management, or any sound information system for its basis. Like him, they faced a general ignorance of what good practice might be. The ultimate task, however, was closer to Church's topic: the issue was the coordination of the firm as a whole, toward a specific goal. But where Church sought to coordinate a single factory, the cousins had 31 factories, producing three main product lines (by-products constituted other, ancillary products). The product lines were sufficiently different, the markets and raw materials sufficiently diverse, to multiply the coordinating effort required manifold.

The Initial Administrative Structure

The successful acquisition of Laflin & Rand meant that Pierre and Coleman were free to carry forward their plans to reorganize explosives manufacture and sales in a large, centrally coordinated firm offering a full line of products. Production had to be rationalized, inefficient plants eliminated, and so on, of course. But to achieve economies of scale or coordinated administration, systematic information was required. The figures in the Laflin & Rand books dramatically underlined the dearth of sound financial information in the explosives industry in 1902. Neither Du Pont nor Laflin & Rand, the two premier concerns of the industry, had any reasonable idea of their assets' worth, let alone of the costs of production or the actual demand for their products. Certainly neither company had any mechanism other than sheer autocracy for controlling expenditures; and

TABLE 2.1

Lafkin & Rand Treasurer's Statement—June 30th, 1902, and Pierre du Pont's Re-evaluation

ASSETS			EVALUATION	RE-EVALUATION
Passaic Mill Plant			25,000.00	250,000.00
Pompton Mill Plant			25,000.00	400,000.00
New Platteville Mill Plant			25,000.00	200,000.00
Cherokee Mill Plant			25,000.00	175,000.00
Empire Mill Plant			5,000.00	75,000.00
Orange Mill Plant			5,000.00	75,000.00
Old Platteville Mills Plant			1,000.00	
Schaghticoke Real Estate			100.00	
			$111,100.00	1,175,000.00
Eastern Dynamite Stock	5761	Shs.	180,869.34	806,540.00
The Moosic Powder Co.	1410	"	98,930.00	465,300.00
Equitable Powder Mfg. Co.	192	"	41,491.35	57,600.00
Oriental Powder Mills	1223	"	50,000.00	134,530.00
Lake Superior Powder Co.	826	"	20,532.50	61,950.00
Schaghticoke Powder Co.	779	"	19,475.00	77,900.00
Laflin Powder Mfg. Co.	2091	"	27,950.00	31,365.00
Chattanooga Powder Co.	544	"	21,760.00	48,960.00
Ohio Powder Co.	224	"	11,200.00	47,040.00
Mahoning Powder Co.	500	"	12,500.00	50,000.00
Birmingham Powder Co.	149	"	5,600.00	14,900.00
The Hecla Powder Co.	157	"	1,000.00	1,000.00
Anthracite Powder Co.	125	"	1,000.00	1,000.00
Marcellus Powder Co.	179	"	179.00	8,950.00
King Mercantile Co.	121	"	100.00	12,100.00
Eastern Fibre Ware Co. Subscribed $10,000.00			100.00	100.00
Laflin & Rand Powder Co.	200	"	1,000.00	20,000.00
The Utah Powder Co.	1569	$5.00 shs.	10.00	00
Driggs, Seabury Gun & Am. Co.	250	Pfd.		00
	125	Com.	10.00	00
Standard Cartridge Co.	243	shs.	10.00	00
Phoenix Powder Mfg. Co.	2099	"	2,099.00	00
Globe Powder Co.	1	"	10.00	00
Indiana Powder Co.	476	"	98,297.82	98,297.82
Northwestern Powder Co.	143	"	28,672.65	28,672.65
Shenandoah Powder Co. Purchase			7,500.00	7,500.00
Southern Indiana Powder Co. "			3,084.89	00
			633,381.55	1,973,705.47

INVESTMENT, INSURANCE & ACCIDENT FUND		
Cincin. Ind. St. L. & Chi. 4% Bonds		
5 Bonds $5000. ea. 94.93 taken at par	25,000.00	25,625.00
Western Penna. R. R. Co. 4% Gold Bonds		
25 bonds $1000. ea. cost 99.75 at par	25,000.00	20,000.00
	50,000.00	50,625.00

OTHER INVESTMENTS		
Pittsburgh, McKeesport & Youghioghenny R.R. Stock		
1000 shs. $50. ea. cost $58.25 taken at 57.47	57,470.00	57,470.00
Morris & Essex E. E. Extension Stock		
100 shs. $100. ea. cost $102.50 taken at par	10,000.00	10,250.00
Jackson, Lansing & Saginaw R.R. Stock		
300 shs. $100.oo ea. cost $72.50 at cost	21,750.00	21,750.00
Calumet & Hecla Mining Co. Stock		
100 shs. $25. ea. cost $256.377 at cost	25,637.70	55,000.00
		144,470.00

*Taken from Alfred D. Chandler, Jr., and Stephen Salsburg, Pierre S. du Pont and the Making of the Modern Corporation (Harper and Row, New York: 1971), p. 67.

each was far beyond the abilities of any single individual, even a Colonel Henry du Pont, to supervise effectively. In the explosives industry of 1902, as in the metal-working industry of the 1880s, the mass and variety of detail had simply surpassed the ability of the unaided manager.

Pierre and Coleman came to the task of constructing systems for management with background in the most technologically advanced industries of their times. Both had been exposed to advanced management techniques, particularly the uses of financial figures, in their association with the Johnson Company and its leaders, Tom Johnson and Arthur Moxham. Their acquaintance with these techniques was bolstered when Moxham agreed to join them in the new company. In addition, another manager experienced in systematic management practices, Hamilton Barksdale, was drawn from the Repauno Company (which the new Du Pont Company controlled). Repauno had been systematically managed although the rest of the Eastern Dynamite and Du Pont holdings were managed in the old way.

Moxham proposed a functional department structure, within separate operating departments, for the manufacture of the three product lines. The department heads would form an Executive Committee to manage the consolidated company as a whole. This structure, like Taylor's separation of line and staff, explicitly recognized that the overall coordination of the firm was a task separate from the operations of any single department or product line within the firm. The problem was to avoid suboptimization. In the terminology of this study, this overall planning and administration is a logical level above the functioning of the departments, being concerned with overall coordination.

The task of devising a management information system that would permit the control of the consolidated company was new, not in any single detail so much as in its overall complexity and comprehensiveness. Records to track expenses had existed before, but the efforts of Pierre and Coleman marked the first time that any systematic attempt had been made to record them centrally, either for the explosives industry, or for a firm of many factories and several product lines. They also systematized raw materials purchases and control, production scheduling, and capital expenditures. In each case, for the new explosives company, the transition was from no control, or at best the unsystematic control that might be exerted by a single individual, to a company-wide, uniformly applied method. The information was gathered in a systematic fashion, and accounting methods and formats were standardized. As with Taylor's specific directions and procedures, standardized financial records freed the firm from dependence on any single individual's fortuitous re-invention of an effective method, or any single individual's knowledge and memory of procedure and detail. Uniformity made it possible for the first time to compare operations in different lines of business. Once the historical records existed, it became possible to manage by exception—in financial controls, even as in production scheduling or procedures. Taylor's dictum, that without standards there could be no exceptions, is as true here as in the shop.

The abstraction of detail into standardized records made feasible the systematic supervision of many factories by the exception method. It made possible a much higher level of coordination as well, by "automatically" specifying the routine, and "automatically" focusing management attention on the extraordinary, on coordination among routine activities, and on the future. Such a focus is implicit in the aggregation of data, for so much data are gathered that attention to detail would overwhelm. The Treasurer's office, under Pierre, gathered information on all the internal transactions of the firm (wages and salaries, production, sales, expenses, and so on) and on external economic conditions as well. Statistical analyses of these figures gave the Executive Committee more accurate information than had been available previously. And, due to the firm's size, the information was more comprehensive, describing as it did the majority of the explosives industry. Also, because of the uniformity of records and the abstraction of standardized presentations, it was possible to comprehend more. Everything was presented in a standard format, facilitating interpretation and comparison.

The effectiveness and usefulness of the financial figures collected in this manner is illustrated by the company's experience during the international financial panic of 1907–08. The company's business fell to 50 percent of normal during January and February 1908. All during the fall and winter of 1907–08 there had been concern over the need to meet commitments, especially the stock dividend, to maintain the company's access to investment funds. The crucial issue was to limit the fixed expenditures (like debt servicing) to what could be readily handled, even in the midst of difficulties. Pierre successfully created a system to adjust outlays to revenues. The company emerged from the panic with its inventories and raw materials in much better control, with future expenditures for raw materials to be coordinated with consumption trends, and, most importantly, with the mechanisms in place to coordinate appropriations in an overall financial plan based on the company's ability to raise funds. Analysis of trends and ratios had provided the key to the problem; attention to overall coordination had provided the solution.

It was such matters as these that were to concern the Executive Committee. They were to attend to the overall and long-range coordination of the firm, rather than the day-to-day operational details (which were the responsibility of the members individually, as departmental managers). As uniform records were accumulated, statistical comparisons became possible, and with them, overall trends in costs, in overhead calculations, and the like. These developments, all arising out of a standardized, uniform information system and the analysis of data gathered by it, also encouraged the growing professionalism in the Du Pont management. In the old days, the firm had been run by family members, with autocratic rule the norm, in part because the firm had been so dependent upon the intuition, the genius and the integrity of the individual manager. The new system was to a large degree independent of individuals. It permitted much closer monitoring of results without such close personal supervision, because the reported data told the story. Now it was possible for a new manager to be exposed to the system, educated in its methods, and instructed in how to use it in a relatively short period of time. Because the information was written down, it was accessible, as oldtime managers' personal, internal insights had never been. Analysis was more objective, and results were discernible to all.

While the logical distinction between coordination of the firm and the coordination of any single department within the firm is clear, implementing it was by no means easy. Focusing attention properly, and maintaining the dichotomy between operational details and overall coordination remained a concern of the Executive Committee. A number of changes in the composition and duties of the committee were made in an attempt to put these concepts into practice.

In 1905, Pierre was asked to work out a plan to assure more effective use of the Executive Committee. First, a separate monthly meeting was scheduled to consider appropriations for plant, machinery, and other large-scale capital expenditures. Next, members were asked to classify their agenda items as important, general, or routine. And finally, an Operative Committee, composed of the second in command of each of the functional departments and the heads of smaller departments (like Purchasing and Traffic), was to meet fortnightly to consider day-to-day operational matters. These changes reiterated the basic tasks of the Executive Committee as coordinating departmental activities, setting general policies, and allocating financial resources, rather than operational details.

By 1911, Coleman, as president, felt that a reorganization was necessary. The old administrative structure failed to train new managers for succession because operational and policy decision-making duties fell to the same people. This prevented upcoming managers from acquiring the operational experience that would enable them to make policy decisions properly. Coleman attempted to redefine the duties of the Executive Commitee further to focus on long-range planning, while allowing it to retain the ability to supervise operations through subcommittees. However, this reorganization failed. It resulted in exactly the involvement in detail that it had been intended to eliminate, in part because of the character of Hamilton Barksdale, who was chosen as general manager.[10] Barksdale was unable to delegate authority, and unable to refrain from personal involvement in the operational details of the departments, even after explicit instructions from Pierre and Coleman.[11]

> His failure as an administrator was the basic reason for his removal. He was highly competent in supervising personally work in the mills, but he had shown little talent for broader coordination, appraising, and goal setting.[12]

When Pierre again became Acting President, in 1914, he reiterated the need to limit Executive Committee action to matters of concern to the firm as a whole, leaving more parochial concerns to the department heads involved. Pierre insisted that, while the Executive Committee retained broad responsibility, this power was to be used with discretion in order to leave matters of concern to departments in the hands of the department heads to the greatest extent possible.

Antitrust, the War, and Further Diversification

Along with more efficient production and administration, the changes wrought by Pierre and Coleman gave Du Pont a preeminence in the explosives industry. They also brought an allegation by a disgruntled former employee that the company had acted in restraint of trade. In the antitrust suit that followed, the Supreme Court required that the company divide its explosives business. Two new firms were formed, Hercules and Atlas. Du Pont was somewhat reduced in size, but its administrative structure and organization remained intact.

The basic message in the Court's decision was clear: further growth must be outside the explosives industry. While World War I brought an enormous expansion of the company and its military munitions business, together with substantial profits, this message was surely corroborated by Congressional riders to appropriations bills which at first prohibited the awarding of munitions contracts to "any Trust." These riders were specifically aimed at Du Pont, although the reorganization carried out by Coleman and Pierre clearly created a coordinated central administration for the firm, rather than the mechanisms of a trust.

At the close of the war, disarmament brought the collapse of the munitions business. With substantial wartime profits to redeploy, and expansion in the explosives industry effectively curtailed by the anti-trust decision, Du Pont felt renewed pressure to diversify. The institutional means of acquiring new tasks and skills, which, in turn, would be reduced to system, fell to the Development Department, under the direction of the Executive Committee. As far back as 1908, the Development Department had been instructed to evaluate alternative uses for the smokeless plants under the threat of excess capacity. Excess capacity was again a motivating factor in postwar diversification, but with a change. As Chandler notes:

> In 1917, the [Development] Department began to consider its resources as more than physical plant and facilities. Its planners began to think about the use of its laboratories, its sales organization, and particularly, its personnel trained in the complex processes of nitrocellulose technology and in the administration of great numbers of men and large amounts of money and materials.[13]

This changed perspective led the company into paint, dyestuffs, and synthetic fabrics, among other new products. These businesses were not immediately successful, however. The dyestuffs business (which the company entered contrary to the initial recommendation of the Development Department) continued to lose money until well after the war. And, for a time, Du Pont lost money on every can of paint it sold, despite its apparent advantages of size and integration in providing raw materials.

The central thesis of Chandler's discussion of Du Pont's diversification, in *Strategy and Structure*, is that the strategy of diversification required a multidivisional structure for success. The diverse product lines manufactured by the company made the old functional organization ineffective and inefficient: critical tasks were different in the different lines. Thus, for instance, the statistics eloquently pointed out that Du Pont made a profit in the bulk portions of its businesses (like explosives) and lost money on the merchandising portion of its businesses.

From another point of view, it may be argued that Du Pont's institutional mechanism for acquiring new businesses, new skills, or new product lines was at fault. The separation of new ventures as the responsibility of a Development Department encouraged thinking about such business as purely an add-on, rather than as an alternative venture. It also increased the difficulty of transfer when the new venture was to be established as part of an on-going product line. Along the same lines, although the structure of the Executive Committee discouraged discussion of departmental matters, after many changes the structure still did not facilitate the overall coordinative view. This might well be discussed in terms of lateral relations at the departmental level and hierarchies of logic in the relation of the committee to the departments. The route chosen by Du Pont was a multidivisional structure, which has become the standard for large, diversified firms. The changes in the Executive Committee and top management structure, which Chandler outlines, included the explicit segregation of top-level coordination of the firm from operational duties at the department level. No member of the reconstituted Executive Committee was to be a departmental head, and the Executive Committee would concentrate on the administration of the company as a whole. By virtue of its membership, the committee would be able to discuss departmental matters at the appropriate level of abstraction, and in the appropriate, company-wide perspective should the need arise. The separation from functional areas was further emphasized by making the recommendations of the committee members purely advisory. Each of the divisions was autonomous in its relations with the others, and had a central office to coordinate the functional departments it contained. The new structure thus provided for several central offices, one for each line of business, with an overall central office to coordinate the whole.

By this time, however, the businesses were essentially set: the "decentralized" divisional structure was essentially a mechanism for coordinating already established lines of business. Responsibility for the acquisition of new skills remained a centralized function. The achievement of Du Pont was to organize systematically one level above the individual plant or factory, creating the information systems that permitted "management by exception" and, for the first time, systematic forward planning and proaction.

GENERAL MOTORS

The essential task of setting up an administrative system to coordinate several related but different lines of business occurred also at General Motors. Under William C. Durant, General Motors had grown to an aggregation of different plants manufacturing everything from entire automobiles (Buick, Oakland, Cadillac, and even Cartercar) to components. The lines competed; there were no mechanisms for communication, let alone coordination among them. Financial controls were completely lacking. Durant's focus had been upon acquisition and expansion, rather than upon consolidation or administration. Those tasks fell to Pierre du Pont, called in at the behest of the financial backers of the stricken company when Durant's personal fortune proved insufficient,* and to Alfred P. Sloan, Jr.

The task of reorganizing GM was complicated by crisis. Alfred P. Sloan, Jr., described GM's situation at the close of 1920:

> The automobile market had nearly vanished and with it our income. Most of our plants and those of the industry were shut down or assembling a small number of cars out of semifinished materials in the

---

*For complete details, the reader is again referred to Chandler and Salsbury's *Pierre S. du Pont and the Making of the Modern Corporation*, and Alfred P. Slaon's *My Years with GM*. Of necessity, my presentation is substantially abbreviated.

> plants. We were loaded with high-priced inventory and commitments at the old inflated price level. We were short of cash. We had a confused product line. There was a lack of control and of any means of control in operations and figures. In short, there was just about as much crisis, inside and outside, as you could wish for if you liked that sort of thing.[14]

Sloan suggested that the task of reorganizing GM differed in some important respects from that of reorganizing Du Pont because the Du Pont factories had been run on a centralized, even authoritarian, basis before the advent of systematic management practice. However, the many factories and companies combined by the cousins into the new Du Pont Company had no such tradition of centralized management. In this, the tasks at Du Pont and GM were similar. Too, Du Pont (outside perhaps Repauno) simply had no mechanism for control or information collecting: the great disparity between balance sheet worth and the value of the properties acquired underlines this absence of adequate information. General Motors and Du Pont were identical, before reorganization, in their lack of comprehensive, comparable financial information, or indeed, of almost any financial information.*

After a brief centralized administration, to carry the firm past the immediate crisis, Pierre du Pont, Sloan, and the financial organizers—many of them former Du Pont personnel, like John Pratt, John J. Raskob, and Donaldson Brown—sought to establish a more regularized organization. Sloan was strong for decentralization, but equally strong on the need for information and the kinds of controls that had been established at Du Pont: uniform accounting procedures, and the collection of information on all the relevant aspects of business. These included expenditures, production, purchasing, inventories of all sorts, cash flows, and, importantly, return on investment. The idea was to enable the parent corporation to make comparisons, to monitor, and to garner the advantages of delegating without incurring the costs of financial chaos, as under Durant. Sloan recognized early that "the corporation could not continue to grow and survive unless it was better organized."[15]

Financial controls at GM had to deal with three critical and interrelated problems: appropriations over-runs, runaway inventory, and a cash shortage. Each was symptomatic of the underlying dearth of information. Appropriations control, for instance, was simply nonexistent at General

---

*Sloan points out that "Du Pont executives had been working on their own reorganization problem for a couple of years; but it was not until nine months after General Motors adopted its plan of organization that the du Pont Company also adopted a decentralized scheme. The two plans did not share their particulars, but only the management philosophy of decentralization." P. 50.

Motors prior to 1921. Monies were granted virtually on request. With inflation, over-runs were frequent—but always covered by the corporation. The Executive Committee was busily expanding GM in as many directions as the committee had members, with no attempt to coordinate. Rather than confining expansion to a few fields, or setting a budget for capital investment, the problem was structured as one of raising more money when over-runs and multiple allocations used up available funds. Without information, one committee member's preference or plea was as good as another's:

> The important thing was that no one knew how much was being contributed—plus or minus—by each division to the common good of the corporation. And since, therefore, no one knew, or could prove, where efficiencies and inefficiencies lay, there was no objective basis for the allocation of new investment.[16]

In the absence of information, no effective control was possible.

The competition for resource allocation was the mirror of product-line competition in the market. Overlapping product lines had to be condensed, and missing elements added (much as Du Pont added dynamite) to fill out the line. The rationale for such decisions, however, was lacking until proper information could be gathered. In unbounded optimism and with no regard to usage rates, the divisions seemed almost in competition to pile up inventories. The cash shortage, clearly made up of appropriations over-runs and heavy inventories, was only exacerbated by the absence of other coordinating and controlling mechanisms. There was, for instance, no means of routinely transferring funds among divisions or from the divisions where sales revenues were received to the corporation.

The coordination achieved by uniform and systematically applied financial controls extended far beyond the strictly financial. What Sloan had learned at Hyatt Bearing and United Motors, and what Pierre du Pont, Raskob, and Brown had learned at Du Pont was a systematic viewpoint that related these various matters. In designing the controls for GM, they consciously sought to institutionalize their insights, and to generalize the points of view that facilitated coordination. Inventory controls, the promulgation of rules and procedures governing production scheduling and the like were explicitly seen, by Sloan at least, as means of transferring the actual control out of the divisions and down into the organization structure. By providing an abstracted measure of results and a monitor on process, the rules simplified enormously the task of top management. Thus Sloan and Donaldson Brown explicitly saw rules and procedures applied by the division executives as a substitute for the centralized control of the emergency period. One might add, they saw decentralized control as preferable.

> The operating units themselves must of necessity be looked to as the primary seat of control of inventories. The interposition of an Inventories Committee [the emergency expedient], with its delegated powers in the direction of inventory control affords a condition of dual responsibility which in normal conditions is unwholesome and objectionable.[17]

The importance of the administrative systems—financial controls, inventory control procedures, standardized accounting methods and report forms, and data gathering procedures—is not to be underestimated as a substitute and surrogate for the close supervision and detailed control of task that it supersedes. Where the old Du Pont Company relied on the personal control of Colonel Henry, General Motors simply left these matters in the hands of division executives prior to the imposition of controls in 1923–24. The new controls, based on standard procedures and detailed information, allowed monitoring of the *results*.

> It was on the financial side that the last necessary key to decentralization with coordinated control was found. That key, in principle, was the concept that, if we had the means to review and judge the effectiveness of operations, we could safely leave the prosecution of those operations to the men in charge of them.[18]

The first step, uniform internal control, was refined with the addition of external information on new car sales and dealer inventories and by a comprehensive comparison measure of the rate of return calculation.

Donaldson Brown defined rate of return as profit margin multiplied by the rate of turnover of invested capital. Each component was broken down into further detail to illuminate the profit and loss dynamics. Sloan commented that this was:

> a case, you might say, of aggregating and deaggregating figures to bring about a recognition of the structure of profit and loss in operations. Essentially it was a matter of making things visible. The unique thing was that it made possible the creation, based on experience, of detailed standards or yardsticks for working-capital and fixed-capital requirements and for the various elements of cost.[19]

Division managers were required to submit monthly reports of operating results. These were put onto standard forms by the corporate financial staff "in such a way as to provide the standard basis for measuring divisional performance in terms of return on investment."[20] These figures were constantly studied by top management, and if results were not satisfactory, they were discussed with the division managers by Sloan himself or another general executive.

It is important to note here that, beyond creating a data base, historical records of performance, and the like, the control tool generalized a way of thinking about results—in comparative terms, in terms of the ratios the form computed, and the like. Surely no manager who had once been confronted by the president of General Motors was likely to ignore statistics like these afterwards. Indeed, the figures created both expectations in terms of results and the format by which to interpret them.

> The early return-on-investment form, which with some modifications is still used in General Motors, was the first step in educating our operating personnel in the meaning and importance of rate-of-return as a standard of performance. It provided executives with a quantitative basis for sound decision making. . . . But what is equally important, the uniform accounting practice created guidelines . . . for overhead cost accounting, both for actual costs of production and for developing yardsticks for evaluating operating efficiency.[21]

The controls that Sloan and the Du Pont team established were essentially a series of interrelated mechanisms for supervising the on-going business of the firm. The major difference between Du Pont's situation and GM's, as far as controls were concerned, was that GM's business was so volatile as to demand much greater emphasis on external conditions, like sales to the ultimate customer (which of course depended on the state of the economy and on disposable income), than industrial products sales. The usefulness of GM's administrative systems for on-going business in changing conditions is apparent in the firm's depression results. In 1932, General Motors' U.S. and Canadian volume was 50 percent less than 1931's, and 72 percent below 1929's. But the firm stayed in the black.

Two key points emerge here. First, a *method*—generalized knowledge *about* the task, rather than task specifics—was institutionalized in the required forms, reporting relationships, and so on. Second, by decentralizing and delegating, this generalized method tended to restrict top management attention to higher levels of abstraction, to the relationships among the data and to refinements of the method. Operating details were no longer top management's concern; they were left to divisional executives. Top-level attention at GM (as at Du Pont) was focused on coordination among the divisions. Sloan was far above the concrete details of the tasks (though these in turn might well be specified by some Taylor-like system) and above even their coordination in a single operation, a single automobile, or even a single division.

Each step in this progression up the hierarchy of coordination represents a logical distinction. Each higher level was progressively more inclusive, taking into account not only the results of several distinct divisions, but also relations among them. That is, each step took into account the system of logic which incorporated the subordinate elements. Where Taylor was concerned with the coordination of the elements of a single task, or occasionally with the flow of work in a single transformation process, Church was concerned with coordinating the many processes of an entire factory. Where Church coordinated a single-plant firm, Du Pont and GM were concerned with coordinating the multiple activities of many plants making different products. The systems of coordinated controls and committees, and hierarchies of information aggregated to permit abstraction, all contributed to a systematic method of managing on-going business, the routine undertaking of the complex modern corporation.

General Motors and Change

General Motors also faced external environments which demanded more than the steady state. The crisis of 1920 involved uncontrolled short-term expenditures and appropriations. The crisis of 1924, which occurred despite good controls in these areas, underlined the importance of flexibility and a proactive stance that would enable the corporation to foresee and avoid crises, rather than merely to retrench to meet them. By December 1923, GM was already basing production schedules on sales forecasts by division executives. Moreover, three estimates were submitted. "Pessimistic" estimates represented minimum expectations; "conservative" estimates indicated what was likely; and "optimistic" were the highest expectations. However, because 1923 had been such a good year, even the "conservative" estimates were relatively optimistic. In addition, in 1923 many divisions had found themselves unable to meet unexpected demand. To avoid this difficulty in what they hoped would be another banner year, the division executives urged the Executive Committee to authorize production for inventory on the basis of forecasts. However, 1924 expectations did not materialize and sales were off substantially. The firm cut back production and sent Sloan and Donaldson Brown on an extended tour to see personally the state of dealer inventories. Everywhere inventories were excessive, so Sloan ordered further cutbacks.

In the investigation that followed, the need for more effective forecasts and forward planning methods became apparent. Until about July 1924, GM had considered disposal, or output, as simply delivery to the dealer or distributor, not delivery to the ultimate customer. Data on customer demand was available, but had not been integrated into the production-scheduling problem. Now general economic forecasts, as well as rationally developed estimates of total consumer demand in any given price range, were to be included. Thus in 1924, for the first time GM limited its production on the basis not only of the experience of the past, but also on predictions about the future. The merging of short-lead indicators (such as

INDUS

Mr. _____

Please Ship to_____ Duquesne University Library

Destination _____ Pittsburgh

No. PACKAGES	DESCRIPTION
1	Institutionalizing Innovatic

ITEMIZED CONTENTS OF PACKAGES ARE AS FOLLOWS

FORM 320 REV. 1-1-65 MISCELLANEOUS SHIPPING MEMO

Date _____ FEb. 24 _____ 19 82

_____ State __ PA 15219

	WEIGHT	GIVE REASON FOR SHIPPING
linek		Interlibrary loan
		on book

HOW	Freight or Express
Car Initial	Car No.
Their Order No.	
Return on our Order No.	
Labor Charges, Cost of Shipping, Loading, etc.	
Requested by	109-T-1 Hazel Green

actual automobile registrations, or dealer sales for the last ten days) with forecasts for the year as a whole allowed production scheduling to be much more closely keyed to actual consumption. The new controls increased inventory turnover, reducing the amount of working capital the corporation had committed there. By tying current production schedules closer to the actual sale, dealer inventory was also reduced and its turnover increased.

The divisional estimates of production and demand formed the basis, with general office estimates, for the control of all the corporation's short-term activities: production schedules and associated purchases of materials and supplies, employment, and price (since cost and price were closely linked to expected volume).[22]. These formed a final link in the network of financial controls that prepared GM for a more proactive relationship with its environment.

The marketplace was far more volatile for GM than for Du Pont, but the nature of product change, for GM, was refinement rather than revolution. The automobile had remained rather static until the 1920s. Indeed, Henry Ford's original idea of utility transportation for the masses, the Model T, seemed to establish ultimate stability and ultimate expansion as the fundamental characteristics of the automotive market. After 1908, Ford held supreme with a product that did not change. His volume production, the basis of his low costs, depended upon producing enormous numbers of identical vehicles. Until substantial changes occurred in the automobiles— most notably the Essex closed coach, offered at $5 *less* than the Essex touring car, the open model—Ford's strategy seemed unbeatable.

General Motors' decision to challenge Ford for supremacy, not only in the low-cost market but in a broad spectrum policy-determined line, was based on the controls described above. Close controls and, for a time, an interdivisional purchasing committee, permitted the first moves toward standardized parts and procedures, thus allowing for the integration of production in different models through the use of common parts. In this fashion, the economies of scale that Ford sought through identical products could be had, as well as the competitive advantage of different products for different markets. These changes will not be dealt with in detail here.*

What is of interest here is less the saga of competition in the automobile industry than the commitment to systematic management that enabled GM to pursue a policy of product upgrading, of choosing its

---

*The interested reader is referred again to Sloan's *My Years with General Motors*. For an opposing view of Sloan's "professional management" as well as of the auto industry's progress, see Emma Rothschild, *Paradise Lost: The Decline and Fall of the Auto Industrial State* (New York: Vintage Books - Random House, 1974).

response, and of preparing (through forecasts) to meet contingencies. These choices rest fundamentally upon a systematic, institutionalized *modus operandi*—an organized handling of the routine business of the firm. This is, with GM's volatile market situation, a more flexible situation by far than the institutionalized "one best way" that Taylor's lists and procedures created. For the next step, that of institutionalizing innovation and fundamental change, we must look to a still more changeful and innovative environment, and to more recent times.

NOTES

1. Arthur Pine Van Gelder and Hugh Schlatter. *History of the Explosives Industry in America* (New York: Columbia University Press, 1927), p. 402. Cited in Alfred D. Chandler, Jr. and Stephen Salsbury, *Pierre S. du Pont and the Making of the Modern Corporation* (New York: Harper and Row, 1971), pp. 13–14.

2. Chandler and Salsbury, p. 23.

3. Pierre S. du Pont. "My Induction to Explosives Manufacture," written October 10, 1945. Papers of Pierre S. du Pont, the Eleutherian Mills Historical Library, Longwood Manuscripts, Group 10, Series B, File 5. Cited in Chandler and Salsbury, pp. 23–24.

4. Chandler and Salsbury, pp. 34–45.

5. P.S. du Pont to H.B. du Pont, February 12, 1899. Cited in Chandler and Salsbury, p. 35.

6. Chandler and Salsbury, p. 38.

7. Cited in Chandler and Salsbury, p. 53. No reference given.

8. Alfred D. Chandler, Jr., *Strategy and Structure* (Cambridge: The MIT Press, 1963), pp. 54–55.

9. From the du Pont Antitrust Suit (1909), *Defendants' Record Testimony*, I, p. 488. Cited in Chandler, *Strategy and Structure*, p. 55.

10. Chandler and Salsbury, pp. 308–09.

11. Pierre du Pont, letter to the Board of Directors, Sept. 11, 1914. Cited in *Strategy and Structure*, p. 65.

12. Chandler, *Strategy and Structure*, p. 63.

13. Ibid., p. 85.

14. Alfred P. Sloan, Jr., *My Years with General Motors* (New York: Doubleday, 1963), p. 45.

15. Ibid., p. 52.

16. Ibid.

17. Donaldson Brown, cited in Sloan, p. 143.

18. Ibid., p. 159.

19. Ibid., p. 162.

20. Ibid.

21. Ibid., p. 163.

22. See Chandler, *Strategy and Structure*, p. 553.

TEXAS INSTRUMENTS

Texas Instruments (TI) of Dallas, Texas, is one of the world's premier companies in each of several fields of endeavor. It has successively been an industry leader in geophysics, radar systems, seismic data processing, semiconductors, electronic data terminals, and calculators. Between 1946 and 1972, TI's net sales billed grew from $2.8 million to $943.7 million, a compound average growth rate of 25 percent. During the same period net income rose from $147 thousand to $48 million. Conservative financial policies have encouraged a higher-than-average price-earnings multiple for TI stock throughout its career as a publicly-held corporation. At the same time, the firm has been almost immune to headhunter raiding: in general, those managers whom it wanted to keep, it has retained. The company has sustained its growth and profitability without resorting to outside recruitment for its top jobs, or even its middle-range executive positions. Morale, enthusiasm, involvement, and productivity have kept pace with profits. The firm's reputation as a producer of high-quality technical equipment has been matched by its reputation as a fair but demanding employer.* Inside the company, on lower levels, TI has an excellent reputation as a steady, generous employer, despite layoffs—the first in the company's history— during the 1974 electronics slump in the wake of the economic recession. And TI's salaries are by no means the highest in the industry.

By a number of obvious measures, TI has sustained an enviable record of repeated economic success in diverse, rapidly changing, highly competitive and technologically complex industries. By some less obvious evidences too, the company seems successful. A great number of employees are old-timers, having served 10, 15, or 25 years with TI. Badges are keyed to seniority, rather than hierarchy, and people allude to their seniority with pride. The company cafeteria in Dallas—where the chief executives also eat—buzzes with cheerful conversation and laughter. The employees interviewed were universally proud of TI's accomplishments, and identified readily with the company.

Such signs of persistent success in economic and human terms argue a successful method for coping with change and innovation in a changeful

---

*Robert Dubin discusses varying criteria for assessing organizational effectiveness in "Organizational Effectiveness: Some Dilemmas of Perspective," posing internal efficiency measures as one horn of the dilemma, and societal utilities as the other. John P. Campbell suggests a number of strategies for assessing organizational effectiveness—and, indeed, some uses for the construct of "effectiveness" itself—in "Contributions Research Can Make in Understanding Organizational Effectiveness." Both papers appeared in *Organizational and Administrative Sciences*, 7 (Spring/Summer), 1976.

In both of these papers, and in the literature generally, there is ample precedent for considering a number of factors as indicators of organizational effectiveness, including morale and similar characteristics, which Dubin labels "personnel management" effectiveness indexes.

environment. In addition, Texas Instruments has a consciously articulated system for managing change. The company's executives take long-range planning seriously, and they have devoted considerable thought to how and why the company flourished. Managers were both observant and articulate.

TI's success over the long haul, and the insistence of Patrick Haggerty that success was due to the planned innovation which resulted from the company's management systems, made the company a likely candidate for investigation. Cyert and March to the contrary notwithstanding, here was a company that claimed to plan effectively for the future. In explicit contrast to much of the literature of organization theory, TI's stance seemed proactive rather than merely responsive. The company was systemic in its approach to formal organization and administration, and also highly conscious of its own evolution. And, finally, the company agreed to cooperate.

Chapters 3–5 recount the history of TI's change and innovation activities, primarily in the words of the managers who brought the changes. Necessarily, Patrick E. Haggerty figures prominently: he was the prime architect of the management systems described herein, and is the only source of information on how he approached these problems. Cross-validation is provided by reference to Haggerty's printed utterances at the time of the systems' implementation, to published accounts by other TI managers and by outside analysts, and to extensive interview data from other TI managers. The central focus here is on the genesis of *institutionalized*, systematic ways of managing innovation in a complex, high-technology industrial organization.

3/

EARLY DAYS:
BASIC COMPETENCE
AND NEW BUSINESSES

The history of Texas Instruments begins with its predecessor firm, Geophysical Services, Inc. (GSI), almost 20 years before TI was established. This history is by no means incidental, however, for some of the characteristics of the present electronics giant are to be discerned in GSI. Retiring past President and Chairman of TI, Patrick Haggerty, traced the beginnings of TI's contemporary management system back to the post-war era:

> How did we begin to manage in the particular fashion in which we now manage? No system comes into being in one fell swoop. I think you would have to describe our contemporary system as having its beginnings as far back as 1948–49.*

Perhaps more important for the purposes of this study, the history of the transition from GSI to TI is the history of successful change—consciously directed, substantially proactive, and, ultimately, generalized and systematized into an institutional practice. In this chapter, a brief account of the transition will be given, with highlights of some of TI's successes. In the next chapters emphasis will fall upon the critical shifts and choices that had

---

*Much of the detailed information on the history and development of Texas Instruments is garnered from a series of personal interviews with company executives taped during June 1975 and August 1976. Otherwise unidentified direct quotes by Haggerty refer to the taped interview materials from August 1976.

In addition, a number of published, contemporaneous sources have been consulted, including articles in *Forbes, Business Week*, and *Fortune*, and the addresses of Haggerty and Mark Shepherd to shareholder and stockmarket analyst groups.

later impact upon TI's system for managing change, the OST (Objectives, Strategies and Tactics) System.

EARLY DAYS: GEOPHYSICAL SERVICES, INC.

In 1930, Geophysical Services, Inc. was founded by John Karcher, a brilliant physicist, who perfected the reflection seismograph and its application to oil exploration. Lee DeGolyer of Amerada Oil provided secret backing and served as a senior partner. Karcher had invented the reflection seismology method around 1919, used it experimentally in the field in 1920–21, and steadily improved it, although it was not commercially practical until 1930. Karcher introduced a number of innovations and perfected various devices in shepherding the reflection seismology concept from its initial status as a laboratory curiosity into commercial usefulness. Among these uses were the electrical seismograph, the radio timing of dynamite explosions' underground transmission, and the use of sound waves in the air for surveying position. Since the success of the technique depended on the recognition of different underground formations by the speed of transmission of the explosions' sound waves through the rock, precision was essential though difficult to attain. Even after the process was made commercially viable, the search for improvements continued. Karcher and DeGolyer operated on the belief that any tool or technique ultimately exhausted itself by virtue of its very usefulness; as others rushed to employ it, the original inventor's competitive advantage would inevitably be eroded. This meant that further development, improvement, and innovation were critical merely to remain in business. There was no single-shot route to lasting success.

The reflection seismology technique was a refinement and extension of the earlier refraction seismology techniques. The refraction techniques were an order of magnitude more successful than earlier, purely geological methods they superseded, and reflection seismology was better still. Reflection seismology revolutionized prospecting for oil. Half the oil discovered after the first successful major reflection find, in 1930, was discovered by means of this technique in subsurface structures that would not have been found otherwise.*

---

*Long Tinkle. *Mr. De: A Biography of Everette Lee DeGolyer* (Boston: Little, Brown, 1970). Tinkle gives an excellent and detailed account of Karcher's early work, and of the techniques and difficulties of reflection seismology's development, as well as of the founding of GSI.

It is important to note that these techniques do not reduce petroleum exploration to a science, for it is not exact. They do, however, reduce the odds. According to the statistics of one source, the success record of wells drilled on geophysical recommendation is one in six; on geological recommendation, one in ten; on nontechnical guess, one in 24. Of 361 "structures" located by reflection seismology in Oklahoma between 1930 and 1937, 146 produced oil.[1]

GSI was thoroughly successful and is known to this day as a leader in geophysical exploration. Its history is one of innovation, highly technical instrumentation, and competence. From the beginning (because the basic concepts were new) the firm combined both conceptual skills and the ability to make its own delicate, precise instruments.

In 1941, Karcher and several other of the owners sold the geophysical portion of the firm (which had come to be a separate entity when success transformed the major activity of the founders to managing their oil finds) to co-founder Eugene McDermott, Erik Jonsson, Cecil Green, and Dr. H. Bates Peacock. All had been associated with Karcher in the original geophysical firm. Purchase papers were signed on December 6, just one day before Pearl Harbor. Before the firm had even begun independent operations, a change of direction was demanded by the war.

Oil exploration virtually dried up with the coming of the war. To survive, the firm turned to military applications of some of its geophysical and instrumentation expertise. Some of the same tools and techniques that located oil could be adapted to submarine detection. GSI manufactured and sold Magnetic Airborne Detectors (MAD's) to the Navy and Air Force. The Navy liaison was Patrick E. Haggerty, then a young lieutenant.

The amount of GSI's war-time business with the government was small. Recounting his impressions of the time, Haggerty recalled that he was attracted to the firm by the people he dealt with, and by their competence, rather than by the amount of business that the firm handled:

> They did a very limited amount of work, mostly for the Navy. . . . The part that was important was the submarine detection. They were just *interesting*. . . . The business was awfully small; I had individual contracts that ran hundreds of millions of dollars, and during the whole war, I think they [GSI] did a million-and-a-half, so it really didn't, from a business standpoint, it didn't amount to much. But it was an interesting *technical* problem, and they handled their problems well.

The good impressions were mutual. After the war, the GSI Vice President and General Manager responsible for the military contract solution to the war-time survival problem, owner Erik Jonsson, invited Haggery to join the company. As Haggerty recalled, Jonsson's offer was a contract for change: "Jonsson said, 'We've had a taste of manufacturing at GSI. Why don't you come down and visit us? Maybe you'd like to take a crack at changing the company into that field.'"

The pronounced shift in emphasis and direction was by no means obvious. The entire history of the firm, prior to the war, had been in applying geophysical knowledge to oil exploration, as a service firm that incidentally made its own equipment. A move into manufacturing as an explicit, and equally marketed second competence was a great leap. Moreover, the shift at this point was no longer mandatory, as the war-time effort had been. Haggerty accepted the invitation to join the firm in 1945, as General Manager of the Laboratory and Manufacturing Division, which was formed at this time. Not long afterwards, the name of the firm was changed to reflect the new emphasis. GSI became "General Instruments," briefly, until it was discovered that another company of that name existed; and its name was changed to Texas Instruments.

GEOPHYSICAL INSTRUMENTS AND MILITARY BUSINESS: TIGHT COUPLING

Jonsson's invitation was to have further important implications, for Haggerty was an electrical engineer. He had been a ham radio operator in high school, and, through his Navy experience, had come into contact with the most advanced electronics available. He saw electronics as the most important new technology of the coming decades, and convinced Jonsson that TI's future lay there. Thus he saw the firm as moving not only into geophysical instruments (an obvious extension of their early history), nor even into military contracting as well (the continuation of their war-time skills), but also into the manufacture of electronics equipment in a more broadly-defined sense. The process of implementing this new identity was prolonged. The vision of the firm evolved slowly, and each new step required organization, thought, and effort. Simply retooling to meet civilian demands and reorganizing to orient the firm again towards its fundamental competence of geophysical exploration and associated instrument manufacture took time, as Haggerty explained.

> The *logical* thing was to insert GIS more formally into manufacturing geophysical equipment for others. But there was a big task, right after the war, just in setting up an organization for building equipment for ourselves. There were only 85 people in what we called the Laboratory and Manufacturing Division then. There really wasn't any research.

What the firm did have that attracted Haggery and sparked his vision was a dual competence, in both the new electronics field and in the mechanical, a rare combination in the early days of electronics. Haggerty's Navy duty had exposed him to what was available, and given him a wide perspective of the state of the art. He was struck by

> the dichotomy that existed: companies were either strong mechanically, or they had an electronics operation. But it was rare that a company combined doing both the mechanical and the electronic at the same time. Witness that it was frequently necessary for the radar antennas themselves to be built by somebody else, and then put together into the electronics system. There just wasn't any organization that blended the two. And this very small outfit, because it had been in geophysical exploration, was building drilling machines, what we called "cameras" (which were really recording oscillographs), and the amplifiers for geophysical exploration. They didn't mix them (the mechanical was over here, the electronics over *there*). Due to the temperament especially of some of the people in the electronics operation, they kind of purposefully kept them separated. Still, because it was small, it was very visible to me that you could cut out this foolishness and combine the two. And probably, despite our small size, we could get some advantages out of this combination.

Haggerty saw a technological advantage in the combination, permitting the company to do a better job. By balancing both essential skills, some cost savings also emerged. This permitted the reoriented firm some significant advantages, at least in the early years before others developed similar dual competencies.

The second bit of the transformation from geophysics was a continuation of the war-time military business. The firm had successfully delivered during the war, and Haggerty, with his military background, felt that this was an important, marketable skill. He also felt certain that, unlike the post-World War I era, this time the hot war would continue as the cold war. The United States would not disarm, and military sales would remain significant. More importantly, perhaps, military equipment would remain on the forefront of electronics development. The budding electronics sophistication of the firm could best be maintained and nurtured by a continuing involvement with the military:

> It made sense to deliberately become a career supplier to the military, but not be captured by being a career supplier; from the beginning, we said we'd like to do a third of our business with the United States government; not necessarily the military, although in those days that was the most of it.

To seek out military business, the firm began to call on the services. Haggerty and another TI manager who had been involved with Magnetic Airborne Detection during the war recognized the need for a particular type of recording device, for which the company was awarded an "insignificant" contract or two. The military found it difficult to think of the firm outside its already established expertise in geophysics. As Haggerty commented:

> When we first went back to sell the Navy and others on our doing some work for them, they would say, "What in the hell do you mean? You know you're in geophysics. You're not an electronics manufacturing organization. What can you do for us?"

Things went on in this vein until 1949, with the company concentrating primarily on re-establishing its geophysical business and looking for entree into military electronics. At this point, TI successfully bid on a second-source contract for radar, taking the business away from another, larger company. While TI designed a new receiver for the contract, "Fundamentally we were bidding on already-designed equipment in the radar." Here was a chance to test the value of the dual competence Haggerty had perceived:

> We just did a good job on it. We delivered it when we said we would deliver it, we did it at considerably lower cost. It was the combination of the mechanical and the electronic . . . we were small, we were tightly coupled. In those days, we won because we were small and *appreciably* better organized. Our emphasis then was on coupling the design and the production together very, very tightly. We knew what we were doing, so we ended up generally coming out, bidding 10 or 15 percent under, and doing about what we expected on it. We were not underbidding, we were not trying to buy the business—although I suppose that others often thought that this was the case—but we were literally able to produce it for less money.
>
> We produced the first systems. We produced our own radar antennas. We did some work with Dalmo Victor—they produced the first antennas. Subsequently, we redesigned and did them ourselves. And we've been in the radar business since. . . . Of course now our forte is really designing it all. We don't even try to second source much to other peoples' design, but in the beginning, that was exactly what we did.

The military business kept the firm at the forefront of developments in electronics, since military equipment constantly pushed the frontiers of knowledge. It also provided a discipline, both in environmental testing and in production to rigorous military standards. There were often other ways to produce a piece of equipment, sometimes better or cheaper ways, if only the specifications could be changed. TI managers, many with military experience, appreciated the value of stringent military specifications. Both the ex-military and the oilfield people recognized that the equipment would be going to relatively unskilled operators, and that it had to perform under difficult conditions. They spent little time expostulating. Instead, they bent their efforts to meeting the specs. The specifications "were a good discipline; they were a way of seeing that the place was organized properly, from that point of view," said Haggerty.

But there were dangers to the military business as well, as time would prove, underlining the wisdom of multiple competencies. The Korean war, which broke out in 1950, represented a diversion from TI's plans. With the war came enormously increased military orders and tremendous expansion—along with significant problems much like those confronting Du Pont after World War I.

> Against our own principles, really, we found ourselves almost consumed by our own success, and increasing rapidly in size. The contract we had won for antisubmarine radar . . . we won a number of other contracts, and one-million-dollar jobs became five-million-dollar jobs, just because the quantity increased. In fact in 1953, when that so-called conflict ended, we were billing $4 million a month in the Laboratory and Manufacturing Division. And we had contracts at more than that rate into 1954. Of course, it just fell apart in no time, and we found ourselves billing only $9 million [for the year], when we had been billing at $2 million a month. So we found ourselves with exactly the kind of problems that you will inevitably find when you're completely captured by one kind of activity and something happens to it.

THE THIRD LEG OF THE STOOL

Beyond the competence built on GSI's oilfield exploration and geophysical activities, and beyond continued work for the military, the enlarged vision of Texas Instruments demanded yet another basic competence. "The third leg of the stool," as Haggerty and the others referred to it, was to be some:

> proprietary product in a field that wasn't either geophysical or military. We wanted to add a third competency. Since I was convinced personally that electronics was going to be of extraordinary importance over the coming decades, I was trying to conceive of how one might approach it . . . in a way that would be *fundamental*, so that you could build on it over the decades: like being at the center of a sphere, where there were opportunities—and problems, of course!—in all directions.

They considered making some specialized product: a special vacuum tube, perhaps. They even invented an automatic gain control for seismic amplifiers, and produced a few. But ultimately, they rejected this specialized approach.

So there were two approaches. One would have been to *use* electronics to make products, both for the military and others. We could have expanded our military operation a great deal more than we did. Hughes, for example, chose that route, and proved to be a very tough competitor. That's the route they fundamentally chose. But it seemed to me that we really wanted to do something different from that. We were already started in that, with the military operation, which after all was using electronics. One could hope from it that we would also begin to use electronics in nonmilitary ways. The real thing I wanted to see us do was get into something that we created that was fundamental to what you *do* with electronics.

The opportunity came with the transistor, which had been invented in 1948, but was not considered commercially viable at that time. Haggerty became aware of the transistor as scientific papers began to appear, and he considered the implications of controlling the flow of electrons through an almost perfect, crystalline solid. The project was risky, but its potential was enormous.

It was clear, if one looked at it, that the heart of electronics was the valve that controlled the flow of electrons. I began to imagine what might be there, as compared with vacuum tubes, what might be *inherently* there in terms of reliability, low cost, and all the rest. Of course, it was highly speculative. There were all kinds of people who didn't believe in it—and I mean competent people inside the field: I don't mean here at TI; we didn't have enough people who were knowledgeable that their opinions should be listened to, in that sense. There were people in the field who felt that these were *always* going to be specialized devices. I doubted that; I thought there were good odds that this was going to be important.

As with the military business, TI's beginnings in transistors were slow. "We were pretty busy, with the radar job and all the rest," recalled Haggerty. "In 1949, all we were doing was talking." Despite preoccupation with military contracts, however, TI found time to pursue the semiconductor line. Once again, the firm set out explicitly in pursuit of a new line of business:

Beginning early in 1950, Bob Olsen and I, Erik Jonsson and I, Erik and Bob all called on Western Electric with respect to patent licensing in the semiconductor field. I suppose at first they were just amused at us: we hadn't done a thing, and here we were . . . and we were certainly being persistent about it.

By 1953–54, with the end of the Korean conflict, the winding down of military contracts amply illustrated Haggerty's point about the dangers of success. The company needed other outlets, other fields.

Once committed to the idea of semiconductors, TI acted with characteristic vigor. A patent license was obtained in 1952, as soon as Western Electric made licensing available. Gordon Teal was hired to direct the TI effort. He was a pioneer in grown crystal techniques at Bell Labs and a Texan who wanted to come home. He quickly gathered a stellar group to work on semiconductors, building in the process the competence in materials science research that Haggerty saw as the key to success in elecronics. But "Gordon's most valuable asset was his ability to pick people." He picked good ones, and got them working together, "tightly coupled," even to Haggerty's satisfaction.

> Gordon had done a lot of the fundamental work in crystal growing at Bell Labs. . . . He set up the new laboratories [for TI] . . . early in 1953. We had a working silicon transistor in early 1954. New people, new laboratory, new organization—only Gordon had ever worked in the field before.

The choice to go into semiconductors was risky. To do it with people essentially new to the field, in a laboratory group that had never worked together, was risky. The decision to explore silicon as the semiconductor was risky. The decision to go ahead with a grown-junction device was risky. Accepted knowledge of the time held that silicon was far too reactive, that it could not be commercially handled. Grown-junction was considered a laboratory technique, unusable for commercial production, where some more mundane production method would be required. TI persisted, rightly surmising that, for limited initial production, grown junction would prove adequate. Success was partly luck, Haggerty commented, but not luck alone.

> There *is* luck; it's like looking for oil. You know, geophysical exploration for petroleum—the seismic method—only reduces the odds. Even after you've found the structure, there may or may not be petroleum down there. And it may or may not be commercial; there has to be enough of it. What you are doing with geophysics is reducing the odds. . . . It's almost statistical. If you can do it long enough and do it right, you're going to come out. But at our stage of the game, as small as we were, we couldn't afford statistical performance. We *had* to be right more than our share of the time. We had to have some luck for that to be the case. We were truly very tightly coupled, which reduced the element of luck a good deal—we recognized quickly what was happening. And we worked like hell. There's no question. We worked like *hell*.

COMMERCIAL APPLICATIONS

In the 1950s, transistors promised a multitude of advantages over vacuum tubes or other available technology for seismic and military instruments. Both seismic and military instruments faced extraordinary rigors. As Phipps noted,

> The seismic instruments that they made in the 1930s and 1940s and were making at that time had to be quite rugged. The equipment they made for the Navy in World War II had to be very rugged. Oil exploration occurs usually in the worst places, in the jungles, in the cold North and elsewhere. The equipment had to be transported by very unskilled people—the people who had to haul it in on manpacks were the natives, who'd put it on their backs, they'd throw it around, drop it and kick it, and curse at the thing . . . so it had to be able to withstand that. In trying to use some of the electronics, they came to recognize the shortcomings of electronics then—its inability to withstand that kind of rugged behavior. And certainly they were very conscious of the need for something that used less power, because for power you had to drag batteries around, which were heavy and bulky, and didn't last too long. So something that used less power, something that weighed a lot less, something that was very rugged had tremendous appeal.*

There were other advantages as well, of course. The transistor offered not only its reliability, lower power requirements, and ultimately lower cost, but also its smaller size made feasible a multitude of products undreamed of before. One problem, however, was a general skepticism about transistors. Poor performance of germanium transistors in hearing aids had given the device a bad name, and the limited reliability of the early point-contact germanium transistors without hermetic sealing held little promise for the kind of performance required. TI decided that grown-junction silicon transistors would meet the need. But once a working silicon transistor had been produced, market acceptance had to be gained. While various military applications would be obvious, Haggerty wanted to use the electronics for something other than either military or geophysical applications. The issue was volume.

> In the early part of 1954, I was frettin' about this. I was *sure* that this was a volume business. It was very clear that the silicon transistor would take care of this military, environmental problem. We could probably get started that way technically, in small quantities that were very important to the business at the time. Still, unless you found a way of doing it in volume, you weren't going to stay. It was a volume business, you were going to have to be forced into volume processes, doing things at low cost.

---

*Personal interview, June 1975. Unless otherwise identified, direct quotes by Phipps are from the June 1975 interview series.

Haggerty and his marketing manager, Buddy Harris, concluded that the pocket radio could be sold for $50—in contrast to the $10 or $12 price-tag on tube sets. But, they concluded, $50 was the *highest* price. This meant that all the semiconductors that went into the sets had to be produced for $10, so that the item would go to the distributor for $30. "The whole thing," said Haggerty, "was seeing that it was going to be a quantity business." There had to be some way of forcing the organization to shoot for that goal, some way of reducing the odds. TI chose to apply grown-junction techniques and to hermetically seal germanium transistors for its radio.

> It was here that the setting of objectives, and being small and tightly coupled—without doing it with a system like OST—was so important. How could anybody believe that you could set up a central research laboratory on January 1, 1953, and have a successful silicon transistor only a few months and a year later, February 1954? Who would believe that you could work on a pocket radio, using germanium transistors, in the early part of 1954, and actually have it in production in October 1954?
>
> . . .In both cases, it was what we set out to do. We set out to make a silicon transistor; we set out to make a pocket radio. We put good people at the thing—and they were *very* tightly coupled. And tightly coupled? I was there most every day, Mark Shepherd in the semiconductor operation, Gordon Teal—and we were all talking to one another. The people working on the germanium transistor were in the laboratory, for all practical purposes along side the ones working on the circuits. And yet it was amazing. If you walked from one to the other (if you want to talk about short-time spans), how sometimes they were so involved in what they were doing, they weren't talking to one another. And so somebody had to say, "Now, what are the problems, and what directions are you going?" One of the important things, one of the reasons why people weren't able to make a successful pocket radio was because the germanium transistors weren't quite high frequency enough. . . . The logical question was, "Why not make it lower?" It worked. It wasn't the best—the higher frequencies were better. But it worked, and that's why we had the first pocket radio. Why we could do it, and why we did it for the $50.
>
> The fact is, it was being close enough, and talking, and saying, "Well, what can't you do?", and then saying, "Well, why does the frequency have to be so high? Why can't we stay below 300?" It was true that the higher frequency was better, but it wasn't essential for a pocket radio.

The critical task was integrating the various skills and expertise from diverse fields, getting the ideas close enough together for novel combinations to occur. The same combinatory advantages that Haggerty had envisioned from the joining of mechanical and electronics skills at GSI was also the leading edge for semiconductors, for bridging the gap between the laboratory and potentially commercial products. In the early days, when the firm was small, tight coupling was feasible simply by dint of constant management attention. Haggerty, Shepherd and Teal could all be on the spot every day, interacting face-to-face. But ultimately, this task, like the balancing of essential competencies in General Motors and Du Pont, would require more attention than even all of the top managers could provide. So, like management tasks at GM and Du Pont, maintaining close coupling had to be systematized, decentralized, and delegated. It had to be systematized to record and preserve the successful practice of early, *ad hoc*, efforts, It had to be decentralized and delegated to tap into the creative capability of more managers, farther down in the organization and closer to the technical details. The key issue here (as with Taylor's systems, Church's line and staff specializations, and the sophisticated financial analysis procedures of General Motors and Du Pont) was replication. Taylor sought to reproduce specific acts; Church sought to coordinate the acts of many in a factory. General Motors and Du Pont sought the coordination of diverse activities in many factories. Texas Instruments sought to insure a pattern of thought and interaction, uniting disparate technical expertise, and formally replicating successful informal practice.

Another electronics application involved a similar melding of diverse ideas. This was the decision to go into the digital analysis of seismic data. Throughout this time, the Geophysical Services Division of Texas Instruments had continued the gas and petroleum exploration activities of the predecessor firm with notable success. Available technology—used by the Geophysical Services Division and by its competitors—simply amplified the seismic reflection signals. The signal bounced back from underlying structures and reflected from the surface on the bounce. This created a good deal of "noise," spurious bounced signals which made it difficult to discern the primary signal. The technique was useless beyond about 500 feet down because there was just too much interference. It took a highly skilled person to interpret the recording, to sift out signal from noise.

Information theory work, by Shannon at Bell Labs, and by Von Neumann and others seemed to offer a fruitful approach. The signal could be digitized, and computer programs used to separate noise from signal without operator intervention. The shift which drew on generally available new ideas as well as TI's own research, was a major technical advance. It changed the oil industry over from simple amplification of seismic signals to true processing, where signals were interpreted and noise eliminated. As with the seismic technology of the 1930s, TI had to design and build its own instruments, develop ways of using them, and market them to a skeptical industry. Charles Phipps of the Corporate Development staff underlined the similarities between TI's digital processing and GSI's earlier seismic technology.

There's a thread of continuity here. When they first started, in the 1930s, they had to make their own equipment, because nobody made any. When we went to the digital processing of information, we made our own computers, because in the mid-1950s, nobody made what we needed—so we made our own. We've very often done this, and that acquired skill gradually allowed us to move on into another field, that became larger than the original purpose had been.

Digital processing of seismic information is now the standard practice of the industry. As GSI had revolutionized oil exploration with commercial reflection seismology, TI revolutionized it with digital processing—by bringing existing scientific knowledge out of the laboratory and into the field. Just as Karcher's reflection seismology insights were considered mere curiosities of no commercial value, so information theory was not seen as commercially relevant. Just as the pocket radio required joining transistor expertise with knowledge of circuits; and just as the early radar programs had juxtaposed mechanical with electronics skills, so, too, the digital processing of seismic data required sophisticated blending of programming and computer expertise with nuts-and-bolts familiarity in seismic instruments, geophysics, and oil exploration.

PRODUCT-CUSTOMER FIT:
COUPLING SKILLS AND NEEDS

In the early days, Texas Instruments succeeded—in the radar business, in semiconductors, in its radio effort, and in seismic data processing—by virtue of close coupling. The company was small enough for its elements to be managed into a close fit by simple proximity. From another point of view, it was small enough for the ideas, observations, and projects managed personally by Haggerty to produce adquate growth and profit. As with the details of management in Taylor's times, however, as the business grew, there were simply too many demands for even an extraordinary individual to handle. The close coupling of highly technical, diverse specialists required ever-greater amounts of management. Then, too, to continue to grow, the firm required an ever-increasing volume of new developments. As in the machine tool industry of the 1880s, increased specialization required increased numbers of managers to provide the sheer capacity for attention to detail. Some means of assuring replication of the successful practices of the past was needed. Here the problem was more complex, however, for simple replication was not enough. What was to be replicated was the abstraction of fit between customer and product. Haggerty himself could manage this process but to continue to grow, Texas Instruments needed to transcend and replicate this skill beyond its president, or even those whom he personally supervised. In essence, it was managerial skills that had to be institutionalized, systematized, and formalized.

A key element implicit in the notion of tight coupling is balance. By balance is meant adequate attention to all of the necessary aspects of the business, doing all of them well enough. It was inefficient to expect each manager to rediscover this need as he evolved, for necessarily upcoming managers' views would, in the normal course of things, be limited by specialization. It is here that formal procedures were useful, both to insure the firm's survival beyond Haggerty ("beyond" in terms of capacity as well as longevity), and to educate or direct the perceptions of the developing managers. Haggerty commented on his own early experience, noting the value of formalized procedures.

> I realized, as years went on, how well [a particular company he'd worked for] really had been run in all fundamentals. Things that counted were both very carefully oriented, and managed; not always formally— but there was something there that kept it in line. There was a formalism about the production procedures, about the estimating, and all the rest, which was very visible, because it was a very small company.

Apparent here is what might be called the Second Thermodynamic Law of Organizations: something much like entropy operates to draw organizations toward randomness and disorder unless purposeful, directed energy (organization, formality, and system) is inserted. Formal procedures (as for estimating, for instance) maintain order. Moreover, they maintain order without constant management attention.[2] Explicit here is the notion of formal procedures as a means of insuring replication. What is to be specified (and replicated) is not the answer that will be arrived at. This is impossible under the varied circumstances of customers, jobs, production requirements, and the like. Instead, what is specified is the means of arriving at an answer. Concepts of formality, reproducibility, control, and, importantly, the specification of the "how to" cluster around Haggerty's use of the word "manage."* He goes on:

> Often, as a company gets large, the best the young people learning can see is *a piece* of it. They may learn that very well, but they never quite understand how necessary it is that *all* of the important things about the organization function reasonably well. You can be awfully good at something, but if you're bad enough at something else, it'll wash you

---

*In a somewhat different context, Harry Levinson notes the importance of "how" a job is done in evaluating managers. See "Appraisal of *What* Performance?" *Harvard Business Review* 54 (July–Aug. 1976), pp. 30–48.

out . . . If you're bad enough in marketing, I don't care how good you
are in your technical operations.

From the practicing manager's point of view, specialization carries costs as
well as benefits. Apparent here as well is the idea of *an administrative
system*, a formal approach to insuring that the necessary balance occurs.

Formal procedures, as Haggerty speaks about them, both replicate a
"right way" (as Taylor and Church might have noted with approval) and
extend the insight of the top manager. They create a shared frame of
reference or way of looking at the business. In this case, the insight is an
awareness of the integral nature of the enterprise, which transcends specialized (and consequently limited) knowledge. Implicit here is the assumption that a broad spectrum, inclusive, systemic general management viewpoint does not come naturally to the manager who must concentrate on a
single part of the business. With this as prelude, we may return to the
post-war era and the expanding Texas Instruments.

TI had dual competencies by now in engineering and production. They
had technical expertise as well in electronics, government instrumentation,
and in their geophysical business of oilfield exploration. With the coming of
Haggerty and the other ex-military personnel, the firm acquired a similar
close familiarity with military customers. Haggerty's choice of "marketing" as his prime example of a necessary skill is not fortuitous. Rather, it
emphasizes his perception that TI had good engineering and manufacturing
capabilities in the early days, but needed marketing capability to balance its
skills. The first of the Texas Instruments management systems was designed to formally bolster and assist the marketing focus, redressing the
essential balance.

The Product-Customer Center (PCC) was the building block of TI's
operating structure. While on a higher level the firm was divided into
groups, those groups represented fundamentally different clusters of customers. The basic operating unit of the firm, for on-going business, was the
PCC, a profit center. Each PCC focused on a fit between the product and
the customer. TI's businesses still center on electronics, but are presently
divided by the company into four major groups, more or less according to
end user:

Semiconductor Products—Included integrated circuits, microprocessors, and charge-coupled devices with main applications in information processing, imagers, electronic tuning, and so on.

Consumer Products—Calculators are the major thrust, but automotive products play an increasing part, and the digital watch is important as well.

Government Products—Military and government contracts, including airborne radar, missiles and ordnance, instrument landing system, and special-purpose computers.

Industrial Products and Services—Minicomputers, terminals, manufacturing automation and control systems, digital seismic data processing, and land and marine data collection for gas and oil exploration.

The structure is considered variable. In the early post-war days, TI consisted of the Geophysical Services activities and the Laboratory and Manufacturing Division. In 1973, TI's organization chart noted four groups and 17 divisions (PCCs were not separately identified), although it showed five officers holding the title of Group Vice-President. In 1961, TI counted "about 50" in PCCs; in 1965, there were 43; in 1975 there were "about 225."

The PCCs, rather than the divisions, were the elements which made up the operating groups and the basis of TI's structure. Each Product Customer Center had responsibility for both profit and operating plans. The manager of a PCC was at the focal point of operations and had responsibility for what TI calls "create, make, and market" aspects of the products. This combination explicitly recognized the functional elements as essential to what was, basically, a small business. By placing responsibility for all these elements with the PCC manager, moreover, the need for maintaining an appropriate balance among the elements was pushed well down in the organization and thoroughly decentralized. The PCC system divided the firm into profit and operating goals, relative to its on-going business. It was a hierarchical system, aggregating PCCs into Divisions, Divisions into Groups, and Groups into the Corporation as a whole (see Figures 3.1 and 3.2).

As the fundamental operating structure of the company, the PCC system focused on current year's business, profitability, and goals. It had a decidedly short-run focus. The system quite successfully directed managers' attention to these areas, thus institutionalizing a decentralized responsibility for costs and profits. A PCC manager was evaluated as a cost-and-profit center head, on production to objectives, control of costs, operating profit, and the like. (A simplified profit and loss statement for operating activities in a PCC is given in Figure 3.3.) Results were evaluated by comparison with planned operating profits. Managers were free, within limits, to make adjustments in the operating budget expense to bring about the maximum profit.

The PCCs varied in size (in 1970 they ranged from $1 million to $80 million in sales). The PCCs also varied somewhat in structure—they contained the basic functional elements only "so far as they make sense."

FIGURE 3.1

Texas Instruments Operating Structure

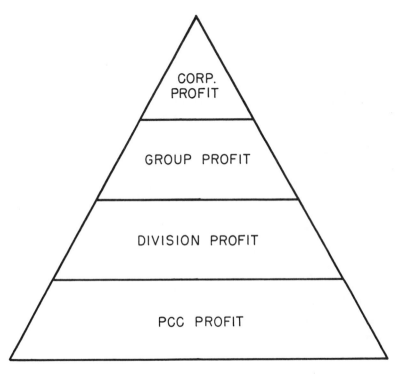

OPERATING GOALS (PROFIT)

Source: Texas Instruments, Inc.

FIGURE 3.2
Texas Instruments Organizational Chart, 1965

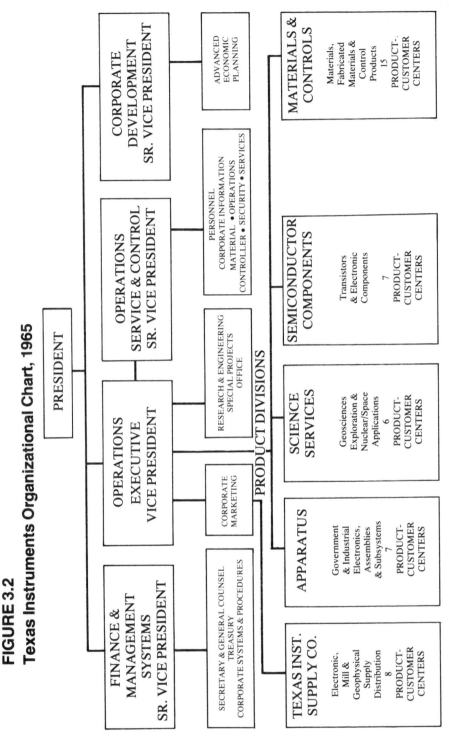

Source: Texas Instruments, Inc.

FIGURE 3.3

Texas Instruments Simplified PCC Profit/Loss Statement

Profit/Loss Statement
Product-Customer Center

Net Sales Billed 000
Direct Product Costs 000
Gross Product Margin 000
Operating Expense 000
Operating Profit 000

Source: Texas Instruments, Inc.

Thus some PCCs bought marketing services while others bought manufacturing from the division. The commonality was that the PCC manager focused on the fit between the product and the customer, adjusting the organization of the PCC to that task. The PCC manager was essentially a specialist in a given market and product who could, when required, draw upon division resources with the PCC budget.

The PCC was a small and variable enough unit that it could adapt readily to the actual character of its business. Through expansion, contraction, and changes in PCCs, the corporation as a whole could adapt to the changing character of its on-going businesses. By virtue of the focus on product-customer fit, the PCCs kept TI in balance, preventing the high-technology flavor of TI's technological base from taking undue precedence in the company activities.

The PCCs, with their focus on current, on-going business, provided the organization essential for what might be called TI's routine activities, those things which had already been systematized. Having successfully institutionalized this type of management, the corporation grew—at about a 20 percent per annum compounded average rate. In 1952, on the brink of its semiconductor involvement, TI had sales of $20 million and profits of $900,000. By 1960, however, growth was levelling off, a recession hit, and profits dropped. TI had achieved the goal Haggerty had set in 1949; it had reached $200 million in sales. But the firm faced a rough year in 1961.

NOTES

1. Ruth Knowles. "Petroleum Specialist for the U.S. Government." Cited in Long Tinkle, *Mr. De: A Biography of Everett Lee DeGolyer* (Boston: Little, Brown, 1970), p. 206.

2. See William Rushing. "Organizational Size, Rules and Surveillance," *Administrative Science Quarterly* 10 (March 1966), pp. 423–43, for a theoretical discussion of this institution.

4/

THE OST AND
LONG-RANGE PLANNING

GROWTH AND PROBLEMS

By 1960, TI had attained the "good, *big* company" goal that Patrick Haggerty had set for it in 1949: the firm was billing almost $233 million and earning $15 million on those sales. TI was earning more per month than it had billed during the entire war. For comparison, in 1950 the firm had billed $7,583,000 and earned $348,000. This growth included some truly extraordinary leaps in sales and profits, closely related to TI's position in semiconductors, as a *Fortune* analysis in 1961 pointed out:

> In 1955, two years after T.I. had started producing transistors in a modest way, the entire industry produced only 3,600,000 units, with a dollar volume of $12,300,000. T.I.'s transistor sales then accounted for only 16 percent of its total sales of $28,700,000; the bulk of that total was represented by military manufacturing, plus a smaller amount from geophysical exploration. In 1956, T.I.'s sales jumped $17 million, to $45,700,000, with nearly half of the jump in transistors. In 1957 the jump was $21,600,000, to a total of $67,300,000, for a gain of 47 percent, almost half in . . . silicon transistors, where T.I. had established a long lead over the rest of the industry. Then followed the fantastic jumps to $92 million in sales in 1958 and to $193 million in 1959. Some $50 million of this latter jump was provided by the former Metals & Controls Corp., which was merged into T.I. in that year; but the internal growth was still $51 million, or 56 percent, most of which was in semiconductors. Thus by 1959 T.I.'s semiconductor business (an estimated $80 million) was greater than T.I.'s total business had been only two years earlier. Profits in 1959 were $14,143,000, as compared with $1,201,000 in 1954.[1]

After 15 years of growth, however, the firm hit a plateau and then a recession. As Haggerty tells it, this generated some serious re-thinking:

> So when we got to the 1960s, and our three-legged stool had worked very well—we'd grown to $200 million by this time . . . a recession hit. All three legs were working, we had had the M&C merger—and this provided both the necessity and the opportunity to look back at ourselves.*

The "necessity" and the "opportunity" were encouraged by a sharp drop in net sales billed and profits, as well as in the price of TI's stock. From a high of $256, TI stock fell as low as $95 in November 1961. Much of the decline was apparently an overreaction to *any* decline in the earnings of a high-flying glamour stock. Even in recounting the company's problems, *Fortune* alluded to "its dazzling career." But the figures do suggest some basis for Wall Street's pessimism. Company predictions were steadily lowered as performance slumped. *Fortune* predicted no growth in sales, and a 20 percent decline in profits for the first half, with the prospect for the year a dismal "no appreciable increase in sales and a sharp decline in profits."

TI faced its first major test as a big company. The crisis was essentially one of success. After such rapid growth, could TI now compete efficiently and flexibly in a highly competitive and changeful situation? As stated in *Fortune*:

> Competition, attracted by the growth possibilities that originally built T.I., has loomed on every side, creating one of the most fiercely competitive situations in U.S. industry today. Any change is still extraordinarily swift in the technology and markets of solid-state electronics, with both components and end-product electronic systems in constant evolution.[2]

Growth was so swift that most of TI's products had not even existed just eight years before. TI's slump was critically related to the semiconductor market, even though the company was diversified into military electronic subsystems, industrial electronics, nuclear fuels, materials sciences, and geosciences. As military spending was cut back, demand for silicon semiconductors declined. At the same time, the recession cut into other markets, and the price per unit was dropped, even as the unit demand declined. The mercurial pace of the change in demand during 1960–61 can be compre-

---

*Metals and Controls of Attleboro, MA, was merged into TI in April 1959. M&C made clad metals, thermoelectric controls, and nuclear fuels. The M&C merger, the only substantial merger undertaken by TI (either to that point or since), added about $60 million in sales. TI was primarily interested in the materials and control products of M&C, according to company sources.

hended with a look at TI's estimates for the year's sales. In April 1960, TI estimated the total semiconductor market for 1961 at $640 million, including military sales (chiefly silicon). By October 1961, TI reduced its estimate of sales to $530 million, with much of the decline in military sales. About 30 percent of this loss was in silicon semiconductors—where TI had led the industry. Semiconductors accounted for about 65 percent of TI's 1961 sales and substantially more of the profits. Direct military sales accounted for 15 percent of TI's sales, while a third more of the company's sales were indirectly related to military spending.

Texas Instruments was not alone in having problems with the industry's overcapacity, price wars, and the lag in military spending. Indeed, while semiconductor performance was "below our plan," it was respectable by comparison with the rest of the industry. TI remained profitable, albeit at a lower level, when others went into the red. However, TI was more exposed to the rigors of the competitive situation because of its significant market share in the hardest-hit areas. With competition from Fairchild Camera, Transitron, General Electric, R.C.A., Motorola, Raytheon, Philco, General Instruments, Sylvania, and others, TI's situation was ripe for a look at where the company had been and where it was going.

Difficulties in fully integrating the newly acquired Metals and Controls—a mature company with customs, culture, and climate of its own, all very different from TI's—undoubtedly encouraged the reconsideration. During this same time TI decided that M&C's nuclear fuel production offered little scope for TI's special expertise. The nuclear fuel business required meticulously following Navy directives as to both product and process. Further, getting into nuclear power in any substantive way "probably wasn't for us." Both of these aspects of the merger must have affected TI's reconsideration of itself and its future.

PCC PROBLEMS

Haggerty set in motion an examination of the company's past success, and its present shortcomings. The most obvious problems had to do with the same factors that had made the PCCs successful: their dynamic, competitive, small-spectrum, short-range focus. By emphasizing the close-fit, short-term, autonomous elements of the company that focused on particular customers and products, the PCC system encouraged fixed-focus thinking about the present. It differentiated the company superbly. The difficulties lay in re-integrating this diversity, to gain synergy and to drive the company rationally toward a common future.

One problem was inflated overhead. Because they were intended to be relatively autonomous, the PCCs tended to acquire specialists for each function, regardless of whether the PCC was large enough to require the fulltime services of such specialists. There wasn't any provision for sharing marketing expertise, for example. Another problem was fragmentation. The particularistic focus that made for close product-customer fit made also for suboptimization. There was no mechanism for melding strengths in one PCC with weaknesses in another. There was no means of coordinating PCCs for the overall benefit of the company. (This, incidentally, is reminiscent of the GM and Du Pont situations.) A third difficulty was smaller thinking—keyed to the capabilities of existing PCCs, or to incremental expansions. As the company grew, and as its growth goals expanded, this difficulty acquired more impact.

Perhaps the most serious defect of the PCC system, however, was that it discouraged long-range goals and programs. Performance measures in the PCCs were keyed to PCC profit and loss on the yearly budget. As a company discussion noted, this led to dysfunctional attitudes among PCC managers.

> Some of them understandably adopted the "Viva yo" attitude. "Viva yo" is an old Spanish saying that translates roughly "Hurray for me and to h--- with the other guys." It is not an attitude on which great corporations are built.[3]

The nature of these problems, and their relationship to the central product-customer fit at the heart of the PCC concept, made it clear that the PCC System was not so much unsuccessful as incomplete. Because it measured only short-term results, it encouraged attention only to these aspects of operations. Because the PCCs were autonomous, the system encouraged a provincialism and a fragmentation (words the company itself uses to describe the PCC System's failings). This was less a problem when TI was small enough for arrangements of close physical proximity—as where "the people working on the germanium transistors" *could* be "for all practical purposes along side the ones working on the circuits." In a small company, one man, or a few, could ask the questions, guide the efforts, question the assumptions, and coordinate the activities of project people for the entire corporation. This was just not practical for a larger firm. The very successes that brought TI to $200 million-plus in sales also lengthened the communication lines, and put more space between more people, who worked on more projects. This, in turn, demanded different and more formal means of coupling information and efforts. To replicate the same success achieved by informal methods in a small company, the "good, *big* company" had to systematize (like the machine tool industry of the 1880s and 1890s). Here, too, the focus was on integration. Dividing the company into PCCs turned attention to the present and the partial, away from the future and the integral. For effective overall activities, all of the company's resources had to work together. In particular, however, cooperation and interdependence among the PCCs for long-range goals and programs was essential. So where Taylor and Church systematized a well-understood business, TI sought to systematize the evolution of new business. To bring off concerted innovation, the PCC managers had to begin to see themselves as a resource pool in common. The potentially divergent goals of many PCCs had to be merged into a unified network, permitting a concentrated thrust. There had, in short, to be some way of implementing policy of innovation.

THE NEED FOR SYSTEMATIC INNOVATION

At the same time, under stress of the recession and the downturn in corporate profits in response to developments in one major area, Haggerty was concerned about a longer-range perspective. In 1962 the semiconductor industry produced two times as many units as it had in 1960, for 3 percent *fewer* dollars. The now-familiar "learning curve" pattern of heated competition, rapid increase in unit volume and decrease in unit price, and consequent pressures toward new developments placed a premium on the ability to innovate strategically. Haggerty had started the company planning formally as far back as 1952, when what he later referred to as "a tough three-day session" hammered out the goals and plans that successfully carried TI through the end of the Korean War and into the semiconductor business. In describing that era ten years later Haggerty said:

> In 1952 we had reached a size which was critical; we were facing management problems, financial problems, and organizational and technological problems of a kind and a scale which were going to require from us a different and more sophisticated kind of handling if we were to do other than simply grow steadily from our roughly $20 million level.[4]

The problems of 1961–62 were similar, if on a larger scale. "Simple, steady" (and, by implication, slow) growth was not enough. Having reached sales of $200 million, TI's survival and profitability in the midst of the electronics recession merely proved that the company "could play in that league." In 1961–62 further growth demanded explicit attention to innovation, just as in 1952 the critical element had been systematizing the on-going, routine business. In each case, the attention of management had to move up one level. In 1952, that meant looking outward to the fit between products and customers. In 1962, it meant higher-level coordination of the firm as a whole, and attention to longer-range, strategic positioning.

Haggerty had been closely involved both in setting company strategy and in monitoring the progress of the projects that had provided much of

TI's spectacular internal growth. "He almost became the project engineer," according to one account. So he was intimately familiar with the past, its successes and its problems. At this point, however, he was convinced that whatever had been done properly on these early projects had to be replicated by others: management of innovation had to be decentralized.

In looking back, his ideas on systematic management of innovation kept focusing on a pattern: "It was examining what was luck, what did you have to do to reduce the luck." Some of the reduction of the luck factor came with a choice of the field of endeavor. This was a policy decision for which the top management of the company must be responsible. It was important to pick fields in which there was room for competition, "where you didn't have to be number one to be important, to make it all worthwhile." This was only part of it. There had to be ways of effectively pushing the oganization to develop the particular skills — like volume production skills—that were needed. And there had to be a way of transmitting the required focus of attention and effort. Perhaps most important, there had to be a way of systematizing all of this. As Haggerty perceived, TI was too big for all of this to be left to serendipity. "I think this is one of the principles: if you think something is important, you had better find *some way* of building into the organization *the necessity* to solve those problems." This meant elaborating a system that decentralized the close coupling, goal-directed innovation and purposeful application of technical expertise that had characterized TI's earlier successes: the Regency radio, silicon transistors, digitized seismic data processing, and volume production techniques in silicon.

The successful early R&D efforts were explicitly goal-directed. Moreover, they were explicitly related to a larger end than their own immediate success. As Haggerty noted in 1964: "When I examine the events at TI through the years since 1946, one fact is outstanding. The R&D programs which have had a major impact on the company's growth and profits have all been successful technical efforts carried out in support of a well-understood company strategy."[5] In a presentation to the 1962 Planning Conference,[6] he had emphasized the same critical relationship between strategy and tactics: "I feel that this concept of strategy, and tactics in pursuit of strategy, will be of . . . vital importance to all our future planning . . ." The critical aspect of such efforts at goal-directed innovation—if TI was to progress at anything other than a "moderately successful rate"—was that projects must be large enough to generate a major impact on the company's growth and profits. These were risky strategies, much like the decision to go into semiconductors, or the decision to concentrate primarily on the silicon transistor, instead of germanium. But they were risky in accomplishment, not in the nature of the goal. The goal was at all times a successful commercial product.

While some R&D efforts might be frankly exploratory—and Haggerty felt that, at best, TI could allocate perhaps one percent of net sales billed to such efforts—the real aim of research in a firm such as Texas Instruments was not the mere accumulation of knowledge, however laudable that might be. TI, as a profit-making enterprise, had to aim at the successful commercialization of some product or service with which to serve customer needs at a profit. Haggerty defined this as *innovation*, in contrast to *invention*.

R&D was not the only area where innovation was needed. Innovation might be concerned with any of the basic line functions of the business: "create" (the R&D or engineering end); "make" (production, improvements in productivity, reductions in cost, automation, and the like); or "market" (serving new customers, or old customers in new ways). Haggerty emphasized the importance of the less obvious "make" and "market" innovations by citing Henry Ford's assembly line, which revolutionized the manufacture of automobiles, and Sears and Roebuck's and GM's marketing strategies, which had generated and satisfied mass demand. This emphasis on all three functional areas reiterated the fundamental balance that lay at the heart of the PCC System.

The early successes had been based on technology, but had gone far beyond that in their applications and in their implications. Thus the creation of a portable radio using hermetically sealed, grown-junction germanium transistors was a technological triumph. Its major impact, however, lay in creating a new market and in generating the impetus for acquiring the volume production skills that would be essential if TI was to remain in the semiconductor business over the long haul. The achievement of a production method for silicon transistors was a technological breakthrough, but its impact was in the generous lead-time it procured for the company, allowing it to exploit the discovery virtually without competition. The aim, in each case, was commercial application. And, in each case, there was explicitly directed, purposeful effort toward a specific innovation. With both the silicon transistor and the pocket radio, "it's what we set out to do: we *set out* to make a silicon transistor; we *set out* to make a pocket radio. We put good people at the thing, and they were very tightly coupled." It worked because people were close enough to force the critical combination of ideas, because someone could raise the critical question. With the pocket radio, it was questioning the assumption that the transistors for the amplifier had to perform at conventional frequencies in the intermediate range, above 400 megahertz. What had succeeded was a combination strategy, going beyond the obvious and seeking commercial application. Rather than *isolating* specialists, the idea was to *aim* them. Charles Phipps described the early insights from success:

Haggerty became convinced that what they had done was the right way to direct and develop a company's growth—to do it on the basis of the technology. They had somewhat surprised themselves: as a very small company, $20 million, with very limited resources, they found they could outmaneuver large laboratories like Bell Labs, RCA, and GE, in the semiconductor area, because they'd just go out and try to *do* something with it, rather than keep it in the laboratory. And they may not understand all the reasons why it works, they may do some of it just empirically; but nevertheless, they'll try and make something real out of it. Secondly, and equally important, they carried it further than the first apparent application. They moved it ahead, asking, "What *are* the ramifications, if this is successful?"[7]

All of this required coordination, above all else. Somehow it was necessary to re-orient the thinking of the TI managers toward a more closely coupled, inclusive, company-wide, long-range view—just the kind of thinking that had succeeded before, with the silicon transistor and the portable radio. The pattern had to be generalized and replicated. Goals were essential, for just as with the problems of maintaining balance, forward planning required a consistent focus. Too, Haggerty had "an instinctive dislike for allowing managers simply to evolve." That was simply trusting to luck, hoping that somehow they'd discover the appropriate path. Instead, according to Phipps, Haggerty believed in setting goals, "usually aggressive goals—goals the organization doesn't think it can attain, to make them strive for something, to push, to motivate them."

Haggerty himself saw the goals as essential, and as effective only when supported by underlying plans.

Now it seemed to me that the essence was quite clear. We had always set objectives. We had defined them rather well. We had set general objectives, and then we had chosen what we had come to call strategies as to what we were going to do to get there. And we set up specific technical programs—mostly technical programs, in the early days.

It was, then, the goal-directed effort, and the close coupling in service of specific goals that were to be systematized into a formal mechanism.

THE OST SYSTEM

The hierarchy of long-range objectives, underlying strategies, and short-run tactical, technical programs was explicitly drawn from the company's early informal methods on successful projects. It seemed obvious in retrospect, yet it had to be formalized: "When you examine it, that's all in the world the OST System is. It's nothing but organized common sense. It's difficult to do, however; it's *very* difficult to do." It had to be formalized simply because it was difficult. The company was so large by now that it was impossible for even a manager of Haggerty's calibre to provide all of the "organized common sense" needed for all of the many projects that had to be undertaken to maintain growth. Until now, while the PCC did a good job of focusing managerial attention at lower levels on the short-range activities, long-run thinking had been left to Haggerty and his top managers.

Haggerty and the top echelon of management could form long-range strategies. The difficulty lay in the implementation, with adequate technical development and support programs—the means of achieving the strategies—which necessarily had to be left to others as strategic thrusts grew and proliferated. In the near-term future assistance would also be essential in formulating strategies. The company had outgrown top management capacity to carry out their plans without the aid of some formal means of organizing the plethora of complex detail inherent in a high-technology, high-change field. The admittedly important day-to-day crises, which affected the everyday activities on which a PCC manager was evaluated, tended to totally obscure long range planning at lower levels. However, in the highly changeful industries where TI competed, the very survival of the firm depended on its ability to continue to generate new products and services, and to pursue long-range programs. This was especially true of the strategic cost-reduction and research and development areas.

All of this came together in 1963 in the OST System, which Haggerty describes as "an attempt to make explicit the company's longer range goals, strategic objectives, and shorter term tactics to achieve them."[8] The focus on long-range aims is deliberately distinct from the short-range activities of on-going business in the PCC System, with which, ultimately, the strategies must be linked. The close focus on customer needs and present products provided by the PCC was supplemented, not displaced. TI retained its basic PCC organization as the fundamental operating structure of the company.

The heart of the OST System was a series of linkages between long-range goals and the shorter-range activities and funding necessary to implement them. The OST's goals were organized as a hierarchy, ranging from the challenges 10 to 15 years out, down to the current year's operating plan. (See Figure 4.1.) The Corporate Objective defined TI's goals in broad product, market, and technological terms. It established financial goals. And it also expressed the company's philosophy, and its view of its responsibilities to shareholders, employees, the immediate community, and society at large.

FIGURE 4.1

A Hierarchy of Goals

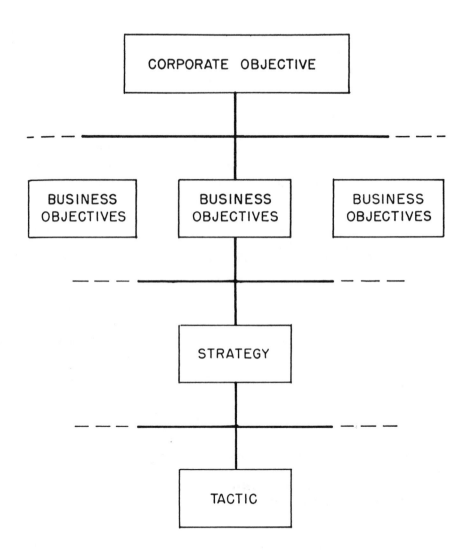

Source: Texas Instruments, Inc.

The Corporate Objective emphasized TI's commitment to innovation:

> We believe our effectiveness in serving our customers and contributing
> to the economic wealth of society will be determined by our innovative
> skills. . . . We will emphasize innovation as the basis for business
> development . . .
>
> (June, 1970)

The main purpose of the company, according to the Corporate Objective,
was to develop the businesses of Texas Instruments through strategic
innovations, primarily generated from internal ventures, in order to serve
cutomers at a profit. While much of this might be discerned from the
company's practice—its "implicit policy"*—it is noteworthy that it is
explicit at Texas Instruments.

Beneath the Corporate Objective, which is the broadest scope statement of the company's purpose, are *Business Ojbectives*. These establish
long-range goals for each of the major businesses of Texas Instruments.
These goals are typically ten years out, with several intermediate points
also given. In a statement to *Fortune* in 1961, Haggerty indicated his goals
for the corporation in 9–12 years:

1. *Solid-state devices*, including transistors, diodes, rectifiers, para-
   metric amplifiers, infra-red detectors, high frequency signal
   sources, cryogenics, semiconductor networks, thin-film memories,
   and the like: "a little more than 40 percent of the $1 billion total,
   worldwide" for TI sales.

2. *Other components*, including resistors, capacitors, motor protec-
   tors, switches, special relays, special controls (e.g., automatic
   controls for electric fry pans, washing machines). "A little less than
   10 percent of sales, worldwide."

3. *Materials*, including semiconductor materials, thermoelectric materials, clad metals, special alloys, ceramics, and so on: "10 percent minus."

4. *Military electronics*, the black boxes and systems, all domestic: 15
   percent plus

5. *Nuclear fuels*: 3 percent minus, all domestic.

---

*For contrasting views of policy—explicit and implicit—see Kenneth R. Andrews, *The
Concept of Corporate Strategy* (Homewood, Ill.: Dow Jones-Irwin, 1971) and Hugo E.R.
Uyterhoeven, Robert W. Ackerman, and John W. Rosenblum, *Strategy and Organization*
(Homewood, Ill.: Irwin, 1973). Uyterhoeven and his colleagues suggest that it is the strategic
profile, rather than the policy or strategy, that is to be determined from a study of past
practice. In the absence of an explicit corporate strategy, other goals will fill the vacuum.

6. *Industrial electronics*, including control systems, electronic test equipment: 10 percent minus.

7. *Geosciences*: 10 percent.

8. *Distribution*: TI Supply: 2 percent minus.

Of the total, Haggerty predicted about 15 percent to be international; it was 12 percent in 1961.[9]

Business Objectives for internal consumption were considered confidential, and included substantial detail as to goals and time-tables. They formed an intermediate range that was more clearly spelled out, defining the businesses through which the Corporate Objective could be reached. Business Objectives focused on a limited field of opportunity, its potential, technical and market trends, and the competitive industry structure associated with it. Performance measures at this level were specific financial goals (like sales, market share, profit, and return on assets) for five and ten years in the future. Product mix, technical goals or barriers, and the likely limiting factors were also part of the formal statement of the Business Objective. This stage of the planning was carried out by the Business Objective manager, and focused on what had to be done to achieve the Business Objective and the Corporate Objective of which it was a part. Any Business Objective had to be consistent and compatible with the Corporate Objective, and with the underlying philosophy and ethics of the company.

Business Objectives were almost wholly goal-oriented. Premises were stated, contingencies explored, and key factors and checkpoints identified, but the focus was on "What" rather than on "How." The Business Objective provided both a framework for directing on-going strategies, and an indication of priorities to accomplish the goal. The formal statement provided the impetus for recognition of "strategic gaps" between present plans and the Objective manager's perception of the need for new products or services. The Business Objective was stated in terms of a "Business Charter," usually worldwide.

The "How" of a Business Objective appeared in the *Strategies* and *Tactical Action Programs* (TAPs) that supported it. The Strategy looked five to ten years ahead, and was keyed to a specific Business Objective. There could be from four to eight Strategies supporting a given Business Objective, and each Strategy had a similar number of TAPs associated with it. Through the 1970s, TI's Business Objectives varied between seven and nine, with "about 60" Strategies, and between 250 and 300 TAPs associated with them. Over the years, the number of TAPs remained fairly constant, although their dollar value increased.

Strategies are intended to provide far more definitive guidelines for the ensuing three to five years. They indicate resources required for an undertaking, the principal decision points, and possible alternatives that might be examined at these decision points.

Tactical Action Programs were the underpinnings. They were short-range, day-to-day programs with current funding intended to accomplish the Strategies and thus the Objectives of which they were a part. Each Tactic was intended to define the approach to a specific action, related this to milestones and goals, and set out a forecast, as well as an indication of the resources required (in dollars, equipment, and personnel). Thus a Tactic was a budgetary request and a forecast as well as an action plan. The budgetary aspect of the TAP was most visible in the funding allocation process. There, Decision Packages, which addressed a 6 to 12 month plan (or, more rarely, 18 months or longer), were considered in support of specific Strategies and Objectives. If approved, a Decision Package became a Tactical Action Program.

TAPs were specific, short-range, operational programs. They lay out a detailed schedule, including responsible people and the checkpoints by which to monitor their progress. ("They're called milestones, but we're going to re-name them kilometer rocks when the country goes metric.") Usually, there was one milestone per quarter in a TAP, with both the target and the individuals who were to achieve it specified. Thus a 15-year goal could be monitored at least on a quarterly basis, with specific individuals responsible for progress at any time.

The Strategic Mode

Strategic operations and planning at TI were not the responsibility of a centralized planning staff. Instead, these duties, like profit responsibilities, were widely decentralized. Each element of the OST program was assigned to a manager responsible for its accomplishment. Typically (although not always), these strategic tasks were in addition to a manager's line responsibilities under the PCC System. Typically too, there was some overlap between operating and strategic activities in terms of product or service. The hierarchy of goals and reporting relations under the OST was similar to that employed in the PCC System, TI's Operating Mode. There is a deliberate distinction, however. The distinction separates out the Strategic Mode—for purposes of supervision, evaluation, and funding. Strategic management is growth-oriented, rather than profiit-oriented (see Figure 4.2).

The net effect was a form of matrix management, in which the PCCs delineated the organizational home of the resources drawn upon, while the Strategic Mode delineated funding for OST operations (see Figure 4.3). The tension between long-term and short-term operational priorities—between today's business and tomorrow's—was delegated and decentralized, with some direction for decision making.

FIGURE 4.2

TI's Overlapping Dual Structures

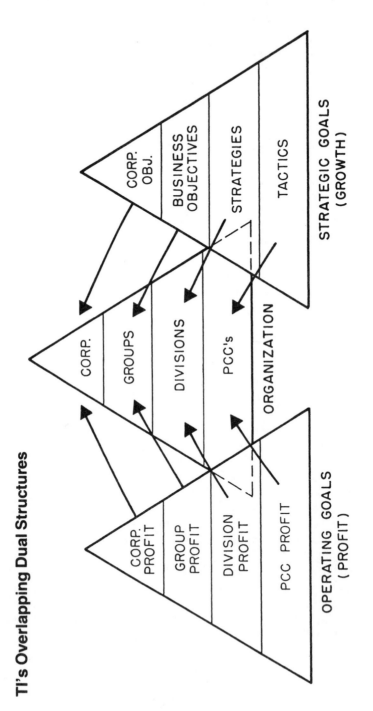

Source: Texas Instruments, Inc.

FIGURE 4.3

TI's Two Modes of Management

OPERATING MODE

OBJ.	STRAT	TAP	GROUP 1					GROUP 2	
			DIVISION A			DIVISION B		DIVISION C	
			PCC 1	PCC 2	PCC 3	PCC 4	PCC 5	PCC 6	PCC 7
1	A	1			X				
		2					X		
		3						X	
		4		X					
	B	5					X		
		6				X			
		7	X						
2	C	8	X						
		9							X

STRATEGIC MODE

Source: Texas Instruments, Inc.

The same segregation was carried through to the profit and loss statement by which (along with other measures) a manager was evaluated. Just as the budgeting and allocation of funds was separate, so too Strategic and Operating expenses were separately itemized. This gave high visibility to both operating and strategic results, rather than compounding them. This is particularly important since the explicit aim of the OST was to fund risky activities, whose lower probability of success, in comparison with current business routine or extensions of it, was balanced by the possibility of higher returns. The separate accounting allowed closer control, since key programs could be given more resources as necessary, without a general increase in funding. In addition, in the event of necessity, differential cutbacks were feasible. Such cutbacks were also definitively the responsibility of senior management. The tendency of lower level managers to economize on long-range programs whose results did not appear in their tenure, in order to bolster current operating results, was effectively countered. (See Figure 4.4.)

The Strategic Planning Cycle

In managing the strategic portion of TI's activities, where a given Business Objective may have from four to eight Strategies, coordination and integration was essential. The OST funding process was designed to encourage this coordination. Funding consideration began with the Strategic Planning Conference, held in the Spring of each year. Some 400 managers from TI's worldwide operations attended, along with Corporate officers and Board members. The conference was a week-long series of presentations by Objective Managers, supported by their key Strategy Managers. The Business Objective Manager assessed the opportunities and defined the long-range goals of the Business Objective. The choice of which Strategies to present, and in which prioritized order, was up to the Objective Manager. All OST programs were reviewed at the annual conference, although they could be monitored more frequently by various levels of management. Video tapes were made of the presentations and circulated to TI sites worldwide, to keep all managers abreast of developments in each Objective, and of strategic reappraisals. This conference played an important part in creating the resource pool of informed managers which the OST System could draw upon, by allowing such information to flow down into the organization.

By the end of the second quarter, plans presented at the Strategic Planning Conference were appraised, goals reviewed, and any corrective actions defined. In the early days of the OST System, much of the feedback was generated on the spot at the Strategic Planning Conference, in direct give-and-take discussion. Even as early as 1964, however, just two years

FIGURE 4.4

TI's Separate Strategic and Operations Accounting

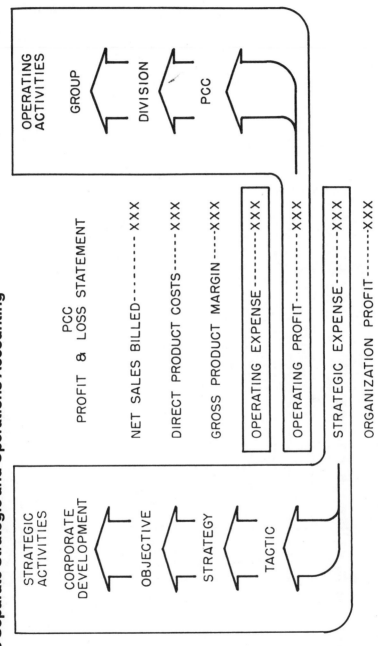

Source: Texas Instruments, Inc.

FIGURE 4.5

Texas Instruments Strategic Planning Cycle

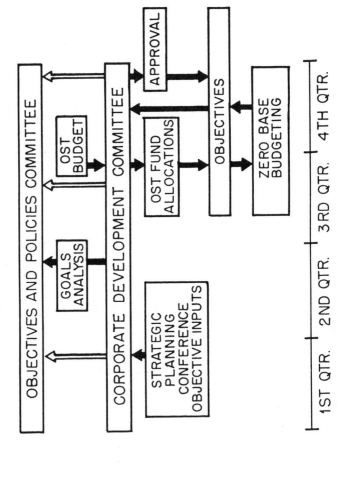

Source: Texas Instruments, Inc.

after the OST had first been implemented, this informality had partially given way to a more formalized review, to allow for both more thorough exchange and more exhaustive consideration of proposals.

Inevitably our Annual Planning Conference has evolved from the give-and-take discussions of its early years to well-organized presentations accompanied by relatively little discussion. The give-and-take now occurs mostly in the pre-planning sessions with each division . . .[10]

The appraisal and review of Strategic Planning Conference presentations was one task of the Corporate Development Committee. This Committee (TI's top agency for the allocation of strategic resources) consisted of the President, Executive Vice Presidents, principal Group Managers, research directors, corporate marketing representatives, and a patent attorney. It met about 20 times a year to oversee OST programs. This Committee's summation of goals and strategic directions were sent to the Objectives and Policies Committee of the Board of Directors. This presentation provided the Board with the long-range and yet detailed information necessary to formulate and evaluate the comprehensive, coherent, overall thrust necessary for the company as a whole.

In the third quarter, the Corporate OST budget level was set for the coming year. The Corporate Development Committee allocated funds to the Business Objectives on the basis of both potential and accomplishment, as represented in revised strategic presentations. Still, at that point, emphasis was upon "What" corporate management as a whole wanted TI to accomplish, based on proposals by managers for what they felt were worthwhile goals, and top management's consideration and selection from among them. Funding to the Objectives was a funding of growth activities in the Strategic Mode (as opposed to profit activities in the Operating Mode). Growth goals were explicit targets within the overall Objectives and Strategies of the firm.

After funds had been allocated, the Objective and Strategy Managers defined their tactical programs as Decision Packages. These were rank-ordered, to prioritize activities in relation to the goals. A "creative backlog" of projects in excess of available OST funding was included along with the prioritized list sent to the Corporate Development Committee for approval. The list could, as a result of discussion with the Committee, be revised: tactical programs could be reoriented, or funding shifted among Objectives at the Committee's discretion. Contract-setting negotiations specified the OST budget available to an Objective Manager, and firmed up the guidelines specified at an earlier stage. Thereafter, through the course of the budget, the Objective Managers were responsible for growth project progress. OST funding approval to that point, and all OST proposal presentation, was done on the basis of zero-base budgeting, thus generalizing the prioritized approach. (See Figure 4.5.)

The outcome of these negotiations between the Corporate Development Committee and the Objectives Managers was an agreed-upon set of objectives associated with appropriate short-run checkpoints. Responsibility for implementation then shifted definitively to the Objective, Strategy, and TAP Managers. Objective Managers were expected to review progress in their programs and to shift funds within their Objective as necessary to accomplish goals. New programs could be started throughout the year, either by shifting funds from current programs, or by an appeal for the allocation of reserved funds. The budget for Objective activities provided a clear guideline for the relative importance, at any time, of strategic or growth activities in contrast with profit-oriented activities.

Implementation during the year was primarily the responsibility of the Strategy Manager. Domestic TAPs were reviewed by the Strategy Manager monthly, international TAPs at a slightly less frequent interval. The Strategy Manager was responsible for maintaining the programs' orientation toward their goals, for facilitating their progress, and for timely response to new developments. Programs of particular interest to top management got closer oversight, but the usual pattern was a monthly review of selected Strategies by the Objective Manager. The selected programs covered key areas, or programs at a critical stage. Highlights of all Strategies within an Objective were reported quarterly to the Corporate Development Committee by the Objective Manager. The Corporate Development Committee itself reviewed selected projects as required (giving further substance to top management's interest in these programs). The Committee was also consulted for the funding of new projects.

Summary

The OST System, then, was a hierarchy of goals linking long-term activities to current funding and programs intended to achieve those goals. The OST operated as a three-level allocation and management system. Goals and Strategies were initiated by Strategy and Objective Managers, generally people with line operating responsibilities and consequent close contact with the operating realities and technical details of the businesses and technologies upon which planning must be based. Proposed goals and directions were reviewed and approved—perhaps after several iterations of the negotiation process, allowing for top-level input—by the Corporate Development Committee. Finally, the Objectives and Policies Committee of the Board of Directors examined a summary of proposals earmarked for approval, for comparison with Corporate goals.

Funding allocations were supported by computer-assisted forecasting, which could be quickly iterated in the course of a single planning cycle. Those who would implement the programs were involved from the beginning. In addition, typically Strategic Mode activities were the responsibility of line operating personnel. The resource pool drawn upon—in terms of personnel, expertise, equipment, and the like—could well overlap the line authority of the responsible manager.

The Strategic Planning Cycle, from initial discussion to final approval, was a massive exercise in communication at all levels and across the corporation. Its very extensiveness marked the importance attached to it by the corporation, and consolidated a common understanding of the strategic direction of the firm.

NOTES

1. John McDonald, "What's Up—and Down—at Texas Instruments," *Fortune*, November, 1961.

2. Ibid.

3. Charles Phipps, Corporate Development, "The I-D-E-A System," June, 1974. Copyright, 1974, by Texas Instruments, Inc.

4. Patrick E. Haggerty, "Objectives, Strategies, and Tactics," Presentation to the 1962 Annual Planning Conference. Reprinted in *Management Philosophies and Practices of Texas Instruments*. Copyright, 1965, by Texas Instruments, Inc.

5. Patrick E. Haggerty, "Management Philosophies and Practices." A presentation at Texas Instruments Annual Planning Conference, December, 1964. Reprinted in *Management Philosophies*.

6. Haggerty, "Objectives, Strategies, and Tactics."

7. Phipps, "The I-D-E-A System."

8. Patrick E. Haggerty, informal address at the Graduate School of Business, Harvard University, March, 1975. From notes.

9. *Fortune*, November 1961.

10. Haggerty, "Management Philosophies and Practices," p. 7.

5/

INSTITUTIONALIZING
THE OST

Within the bare skeleton of Objectives, Strategies and Tactics, the OST is intended to build into the organization certain responses. It is intended to guide the thoughts and responses of the managers who work within it and to inculcate a strategic and wide-ranging viewpoint. In other words, it is designed to generalize an approach that had succeeded among a few managers in a small company to the practice of a large number of managers in a big company. By specifying procedure and the types of information desired, the system encouraged the manager into a pattern of close coupling, of consideration of alternatives, and of goal-focused activity. From another point of view, the system is like the specified procedures of Taylor or Church, in that it provides a formal guide to substitute for the personal attention of top management in coordinating the task-related activity—here, related to the task of innovation. On the one hand, this permits a redirection of top-level management attention to the coordination of many innovative projects. On the other, it redirects the attention of lower-level managers toward the long-range activities hitherto left exclusively to top executives under the PCC System.

In order to accomplish this, top management had to be refocused, from leading projects to managing and orchestrating others' efforts in leading innovative projects. A look at the committee structure and functioning at the corporate level gives an indication of the extent of top-level involvement in the innovation and planning processes at Texas Instruments.

To avoid making the innovation effort an ivory tower exercise, or something one went through "to keep top management off one's back," managers at all levels had to become meaningfully involved in the planning and innovation process. This meant that lower level management had to have some significant say in the process, and that they had to have serious responsibility for its success. This, in turn, demanded that a number of changes be made in the OST itself. Linkages had to be constructed to reinforce the processes and patterns of perception that the OST required. In addition, the OST had to be kept in place long enough for managers to adjust to a new, different, and initially difficult way of approaching innovation. This was complicated by the inherent conflict between short-run operational demands and the requirements for long-term effort. Finally, once the OST was functional, its methodology could be generalized beyond projects of technological innovation.

While all these aspects of adjustment can be conveniently separated as concepts, in practice they were—and are—interconnected. Adjustments occurred in clusters or simultaneously, with changes in any one aspect having an impact on other elements of the system. Thus the conceptual distinction, while useful, is also partially misleading. On the ground, the systemic interactions seem far more apparent than the neat, conceptual separations. Finally, most of this discussion deals with the more obvious, more formal adjustments that took place in the administrative systems (like, for example, changes in the accounting procedure, or in the formal evaluation process). A much larger (albeit far less obvious) body of change took place in the less tangible context of the company climate. This too is systemic, and at once the cause and the effect of the management practices and philosophies of Texas Instruments. Instantly perceptible to the observer, the TI climate is much less easy to capture in a description. Many of the connections appear to be tenuous at best. But the climate contributes importantly to the successful functioning of the OST System.

While the focus of this study is primarily upon the formal systems and interconnections that link the OST to management practice at TI, climate permeates the functioning of the OST. It must, therefore, enter importantly into the discussion. No exhaustive examination of the climate is intended, but frequent reference to it, to informal, attitudinal factors, and to their effects on the OST is inescapable.

ADJUSTING PEOPLE TO THE SYSTEM

The OST System was not instantly nor easily installed. On the contrary, it was a year aborning in its preliminary descriptive phase. According to Haggerty, some seven years of effort ensued to ensure implementation. "It took a long time, and a lot of false starts. We introduced it in 1962, but boy, it was 1969 before it was really working. Except in some places . . . it worked right away in some places. In others it took a *long* time."*

---

*Personal Interview, 1976 series.

Others also referred to the extended implementation and adjustment effort. Part of the difficulty was that the OST is complex. It imposes multiple, often conflicting demands on the managers who work within it. Much of what it demands is non-intuitive, or even counter-intuitive. Yet the very strength of the OST is that, eventually, it generates the non-intuitive, non-obvious perspectives of general management far down in the organization. These perspectives are, precisely, those lacking in the PCC System, yet essential to long-range survival in a changeful environment. They are the substance of a proactive relation to environmental change.

The non-intuitive responses sought under the OST include a view of the organization as a whole as a resource pool to be drawn upon for strategic endeavor. Since most managers at TI have both line operating responsibilities and OST duties, the conflict between PCC provincialism and strategic eclecticism is internalized, and at fairly low levels. Ideally, the OST provides for synergy by coupling the capabilities of different businesses, technologies, and specialties (see Figure 5.1). This coupling takes time to learn. Haggerty commented that such thinking did not evolve naturally in a specialist manager. A successful TI manager corroborated this view in recounting his own first experience on an OST project.

> My first involvement with the OST System . . . was a traumatic experience for me, because I'd been in the Central Research Lab during my entire stay at TI. [At that point about three years.] I'd been involved with research—Corporate research, some applied research and development. Suddenly I was thrust into the cruel world of business strategy and product strategy . . . It was traumatic for me, being a researcher and going over to the Radar Division. It was traumatic for them, having to put up with me.*

The sources of the trauma involved differences in values, orientations, and outlook. Conflicting stereotypes had to be resolved before the coupling could take place.

> You see, I had this image that I was going to have to go over and work with a bunch of blacksmiths. The image they had was that they were going to have to put up with this egg-head from the ivory tower, who was going to come over and waste their profits. It took a year, and it turned out that neither was the case. We gained a lot of respect for each other.

---

*Personal Interview, 1975 series. At the time of the interview, Turner Hasty was head of the Semiconductor Research and Development Laboratory. Formerly he had been at the Central Research Laboratory.

FIGURE 5.1

Texas Instruments: Synergistic Impact of OST Programs

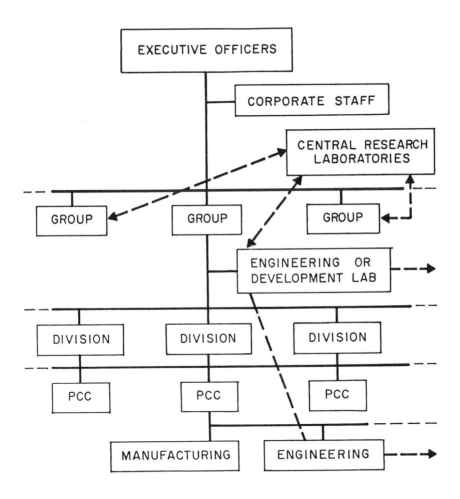

Source: Texas Instruments, Inc.

The orientations were toward pure research, on the one hand, and product-profit emphasis, on the other. To work out the differences, contact was essential. The necessary contact had to occur in conjunction with a problem to which each side could contribute. An exchange of personnel (made possible by the OST project this manager was working on) was the key to an eventual tight coupling that melded different skills.

> I gave a lot of direction to them, and they gave to me, too. For example, to be specific, I had been heavily involved in the development of solid-state microwave sources. And my idea of developing solid-state microwave sources was to develop sources that operated at the highest frequency, the highest power level one could conceive, because that was what I liked to do. I wanted it to go from the microwave range to the millimeter range, into the far infrared, if I could. That's what I wanted to do. And we had a large program [in the Central Research Laboratory] working in that area. That's where we were going; boy, we were really in the forefront. These weren't necessarily the most difficult problems, they were the ones that were the most fun.
>
> As soon as I went into it in the Radar Division, managing their research staff, I recognized that wasn't at all what they really needed. They had already developed a plan, with all the basic elements that they needed, and they had been totally ignored. So my direction was totally changed, really turned around.

The researcher was not alone in finding himself redirected by the contract.

> After sitting in on some of the Strategy Reviews, it was obvious to me that the Radar Division *needed* the type of thing that we could develop. It wasn't as obvious to them: they didn't see us developing anything. They gave me immediate direction: "OK, guys, it'd be just as much fun for us to go back down the KC band, where we have our business." We could develop electronic tuning, we could develop the type of oscillator with a tight range that could meet the specifications of advanced radar.

This was very much Haggerty's goal-directed research. A possible fit was perceived between the skills of the research lab people and the needs of the Radar Division. The research called for here, then, was aimed at a particular *product* need; it was

> very specific, equally as difficult, if not more so, not nearly as glamorous to develop the thing, and it took some hard digging. But it was absolutely essential to some of the advanced radar that we were working on. And I recognized that if we developed this type of device, with this type of a system, that we would enable our Radar Division to make a real radar advance. Again, we still had this gap—this credibility gap—between R&D and the product division.

Confrontation, exchange of viewpoints, and side-by-side, day-to-day contact, created by the common project and the balanced tensions which the OST System had brought together, were the levers of change. The researcher, moved into a product division strategy, was encouraged to bring a divergent view and an awareness of different skills to bear upon the problem. The researcher took action on his own initiative to further the fit.

> I talked the Strategy Manager . . . into sending some of his Radar Division engineers right out of the Radar Division into our group at the Central Research Lab. He did, and that was a very successful venture. . . . We began to set up very specific programs. . . . and we realized that one advance was just getting all of us together. Each one had something to bring that the other couldn't do. The day-to-day contact with the other department was the most important thing.

The product that resulted was important. Even more important, however, was a changed viewpoint that grew from the close coupling which had created the product advance. The particularized "culture" of a given department*—the Radar Division's engineering, or the Central Research Lab—was displaced by a common, more enriched culture. A new set of values, goals, aims, and procedures are the outcome of a successful OST project.

> There was a recognition that we could conduct R&D with a specific goal in mind for the short term, and that it required equally sophisticated research, equally sophisticated techniques, as anything else that we could develop that was more esoteric, that would not ever affect our business.

It is worth noting that what has occurred is clearly a shift, rather than a co-optation: the values of research—difficult undertakings, sophistication

---

*The differentiation alluded to here is very suggestive of the kinds described by Paul R. Lawrence and Jay W. Lorsch in their pioneering study, *Organization and Environment* (Graduate School of Business, Harvard University: Boston, 1967). The "ivory tower" research attitude—"develop sources that operated at the highest frequency, the highest power level"—is indicative of a different orientation toward time, toward the nature of the task (and, clearly, its definition!), and toward the uncertainty acceptable in a particular system of values. In contrast, the product-profit focus—"the cruel world of business strategy and product strategy"—recalled the operational world of profit and loss, commitments, specifics, deadlines, and budgets. The stereotypes—"egg-head from the ivory tower" and "black-smiths"—speak volumes about the different subculture of research and product-division. Abundant evidence of similar subculture identification and differences are visible in the interview data throughout.

in techniques, and advancement in understandings—are visible here. The shift accommodates and includes the profit goals of the product division, rather than simply surrendering to them. The exchange described here was so successful that, eight years later, a contingent of radar engineers continued to work with the Central Research Lab. Their cooperation is so close that "Sometimes it's hard to tell which engineers report to which group."

A DIFFERENT KIND OF THINKING

Adjustments of people to the system were not limited to revisions of stereotypes or goals. The OST aims to replicate the strategic thinking formerly provided by Haggerty and a few managers at the top who personally guided new projects. Changed views of authority and responsibility (different from those prevalent in management texts, pointed out Haggerty; different from that prevalent in U.S. society, commented another TI manager*) resulted in conflict between the old way of thinking and the new. The conflict grew from a fundamental difference between the OST and the Operating System.

> Right from the beginning there's been conflict. In fact, it's really not so much the OST System, or the Operating System that causes the conflict. The real conflict comes about with a person's ability to perceive how he can operate with responsibility but not have the authority to go along with it. This is particularly true of a young manager. They have a very hard time getting to the point where they can accept this. Any time we start up a new business—for example, the calculator business is relatively new—this has been a struggle. And each time we make a new TAP manager, or he comes in to be a Strategy Manager, it's very hard to see—particularly for the TAP manager. And if you ask a TAP manager to take responsibility for an operation, and he does not have enough control to just *order* it to be done, he gets very, very frustrated. It's not an efficient system. It means he has to use every skill available—apart from just ordering it, just like in the Army—to get it done. So I would say that's probably the most common problem.

---

*Personal Interview, 1975 series. At the time of the interview, Ralph Dosher was Assistant Objective Manager of Calculator Products. He was head of Strategic Planning during the time when the OST System was taking shape, during the late 1960s. He had also been Operations Manager for Appliance Controls before moving to his present position. His career at TI included extensive and varied experience across several functional areas (Corporate Planning, Engineering, Marketing, and line operational Manufacturing) and several TI businesses (including Materials Products, Industrial Products, and Government Products).

Change does occur, though it may be slow because of the lack of structure in the OST, and the divergence between that system and other arrangements with which the manager is more familiar.

> Once someone understands this, and he learns to operate it, then there's no problem at all . . . but it's very hard to get all his attitudes changed. Of course, this is a function of the kind of training he's had. If he came right out of the Army, it's *very*, very hard. If he's come out of some environment that's unstructured, very undisciplined, normally he doesn't have too much of a problem. Manufacturing people have it even worse. The manufacturing part of the business is very structured. So it's very hard to get manufacturing TAPS to be effective. Engineering is next. Usually marketing is easiest, because they're used to dealing with very unstructured things. They have to go out and deal with the public, with customers—with absolutely no authority. They have all the responsibility of the whole company behind them. But they can't come back and order anybody in the company to do anything. For them, it's not as much of a struggle.

One of the paradoxes of the OST is that, until a manager has internalized it and begun to pattern his thinking along the channels it provides, it seems cumbersome and limiting. That is, until the manager has acquired the shared frame of reference which is the OST's aim, *all* he sees is its structure.

> Once a manager accepts it, and understands it, then he really makes it work for him, and he doesn't let it get in the way. Up until the time he really accepts it, all he can see is structure; all he can see is forms, reports, and so forth. And he fights it. I would say at any one point in time at least 50 percent or more of the total organization is in the mode that they're fighting. The rest of them have already developed past that point.

The shift taking place here is that of getting beyond the nuts-and-bolts familiarity with the mechanisms of the OST into an internalization of it. This is, on the individual level, the same process the company went through in institutionalizing the OST.

THE SYSTEM IN MOTION

In part, of course, many individuals learning is what makes up "organizational" learning. The difference between individual and group learning is analogous to the distinction between an aggregation and a group; it centers on the idea of a shared frame of reference. What marks the shift from individual to organizational learning for our purposes is evidence of a formal change in the administrative system of the firm. The distinction here can be elucidated by examples of the types of problems or questions at each level. As individual managers at Texas Instruments learned to operate the system, the questions they raised concerned the mechanics of their involvement: "How do you write a Strategy?" "What's the difference between a Tactic and a Strategy?" "How can I manage when I cannot *order* things done?" At the same time, the system itself was being adjusted. Concerns at this level—which are qualitatively different from the foregoing questions—include such issues as the relationship of the milestones to actual accomplishment in a Tactical Action Program, adjustments to the control system, and the construction of linkages joining the OST to the management system already in place, the PCC. Clearly, changes of this type affect the perceptions and behaviors of individuals operating within the OST. Just as clearly, the whole purpose in making such shifts is to "build the system into the organization" more effectively—that is, to strengthen and reinforce the shared frame of reference that the OST should provide. This second level of concern provides for evolution beyond the initial OST System. It represents a concern or an issue *about* the System. From another point of view, each of these concerns might be described as a boundary issue having to do with the fit of the OST System as a whole into the larger task of management. The OST began as a partial system directed explicitly at technological innovation, itself only a portion of the overall task of management. The types of concern visible at this second level have as a focus building the OST into the culture, making it a part of the administrative technology or knowledge of the firm.*

Organizational pressures and individual pressures interact. During the extended period of implementation, before the OST System was sufficiently institutionalized to be self-supporting, top-level management backing was essential. It was Haggerty's personal conviction and insistence that kept the system in place long enough for it to begin to function. Haggerty, and a number of other managers interviewed, commented that for the first few years, "The boys were only doing it to keep Pat [Haggerty] off their

---

*The concept of building "administrative knowledge" of a procedure into the firm, typicaly long after the "technical knowledge" has been discovered by specialists, is discussed at length in a dissertation by Edwin A. Murray, "The Implementation of Social Policies in Commercial Banks," unpublished doctoral dissertation, Graduate School of Business, Harvard University, 1974. A subsequent article, "The Social Response Process in Commercial Banks: An Empirical Investigation," *Academy of Management Review* (1:3, July, 1976) highlights the important function played by chief executives, and the need to build into the administrative systems of the organization changed performance expectations. Murray's findings are entirely consistent with my own.

backs." An OST proposal would be filed, but not looked at again until strategy review time came around. It took several years before the mana-o gers were really *doing* the strategic thinking, not merely going through the motions. The shift took place largely because Haggerty reinforced his insistence. Top management was very much a part of the system, and "visibility"—a favorite TI word for describing what the OST provides— made sure that those at the top had ample opportunity to see who was really doing the strategic thinking. The system was built in, and individuals began to adjust to it because there were strong, multiple signals reinforcing Haggerty's insistence that "this is the way to do it."

In order to get the shift to take place, and in order to get individuals to adjust to the system, the OST itself was adjusted. Its methods were generalized in the People and Asset Effectiveness (P&AE) System. Once the OST had been well and truly built in, it could be generalized; once this was accomplished, it permeated the entire management structure of TI. At this remove, the impact of the OST as a way of thinking, a way of structuring an approach to *innovation in general* emerges. The OST was by no means inherently limited to technology or technical projects; it was merely that its fundamental outlines had evolved in technical project work.

When the OST was, according to Haggerty, "really in," the name of the OST Committee was changed, and the second OST-type activity, the People and Asset Effectiveness program, was undertaken.

THE STRUCTURE OF ATTENTION

If one aim of the OST was to shape the approach of junior management to innovation, another was to focus the attention of senior management. A look at the structure and functioning of the corporate-level committees at Texas Instruments will give some indication of the results by suggesting the extent of top-level involvement with the OST and with innovation.

The management systems of Texas Instruments—initially the PCC, then the OST, and now the P&AE—were implemented within a structure headed by corporate-level committees with interlocking membership. (See Figures 5.2 and 5.3.) Just as the systems create a shared frame of reference at lower levels, they facilitated a shared perspective at the top as well.

The Committee System

The Operating Committee. The Committee that *runs* the Company consists of the president (who usually heads the committee), executive vice presidents, and principal group managers. This committee meets every Monday to review operating problems and policies. Its members serve on three associated committees, with executive vice presidents usually rotat-

FIGURE 5.2

Texas Instruments Management Structure

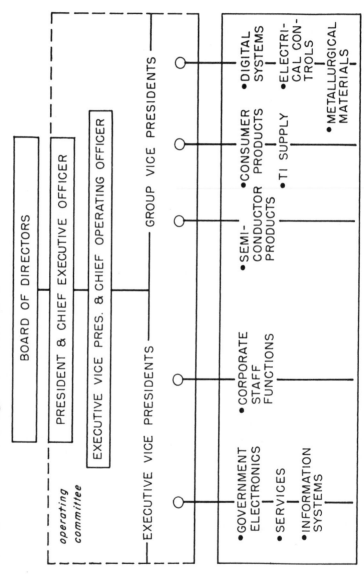

Source: Texas Instruments, Inc.

102

FIGURE 5.3

Texas Instruments Strategic Management Committees

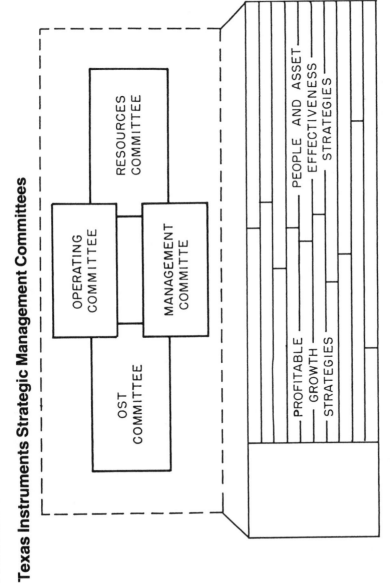

Source: Texas Instruments, Inc.

ing as heads. This committee is logically most closely associated with the PCC structure of the company, and with its on-going businesses.

The Corporate Development Committee (formerly the OST Committee). The president, executive vice presidents, principal group managers, and associated (small) staff oversee the growth and development activities of TI, and the operation of the OST System. This group is responsible for the long-term goals and strategic activities of the firm, allocation of strategic funds, and supervision of Objectives. This committee reports to the Objectives and Policies Committee of the Board of Directors.

The People and Asset Effectiveness Committee (P&AE). The P&AE program, a "major thrust" like growth, is another Corporate Development Committee responsibility. P&AE is identified as part of the Corporate Objective. The P&AE program, modelled after the OST and using its methodology of Objectives, Strategies and Tactics in a hierarchy of related goals, is focused on productivity improvement, information systems, materials usage, EEO programs, personnel development, and the like. People and Asset Effectiveness activities were formerly handled by a corporate level P&AE Committee. Recently, this committee was replaced by a *Capital and Asset Effectiveness Committee*, consisting of the executive vice president, a controller, and the chairmen of several subcommittees (on Corporate Facilities, Liquidity, and Product Rationalization & Capacity). Management and allocation of capital authorizations and funding for equipment and facilities are the responsibilities of this committee. This committee's major emphasis falls upon equipment and facilities utilization and financial matters. Human resources activities—"people effectiveness"— now fall under the aegis of the Corporate Development Committee.*

The Management Committee. This committee consists of about 26 senior managers, including the president, chief operating officer, executive vice presidents, group managers and division managers, senior staff managers, and other key managers. Its activities are tied to the Rolling Quarterly Plan which TI uses instead of an annual plan. The division managers present the results of the past quarter, along with an updated forecast of the coming six to eight quarters. Detail increases as a quarter approaches. This focus is more general than that of the Operating Committee.

---

*Evolution of TI's management systems continues. In 1977, the P&AE Committee was renamed the Capital and Asset Effectiveness Committee, reflecting the source and facilities focus of major subcommittees of the old P&AE Committee. P&AE activities shifted to the Corporate Development Committee.

The Committees in Action

Interlocking membership on the top committees allows for integration of strategic activities with operations, without losing sight of the distinctions. The Operating Committee is responsible for dividing up available funding between operations, growth and development, and resource projects—that is, among the PCCs, OST activities, and P&AE programs. This is done on the basis of successive glimpses at the coming year, by quarters, in increasing detail. In the course of Management Committee meetings, when division managers present their Rolling Quarterly Plan reports, the past quarter and the updated forecast for the coming six to eight quarters are pictured in detail. While the focus is on operations, these reports provide the strategic perspective for looking to the future, and emphsize the effect of operating decisions. The corporate goal, overall, is a 12 percent return on increasing assets (see Figure 5.4). By August, the Operating Committee has seen the coming year in quarters twice (years farther out than six to eight quarters are forecast on a yearly basis). At that time, the Operating Committee advises the Corporate Development Committee of how much money it can plan on for strategic expenses altogether, corporation-wide, for the coming year. The Corporate Development Committee will allocate funds to each Business Objective. While staff and Business Objective managers assist and advise the Corporate Development Committee, the decision is the responsibility of the senior officers; it is not a "committee decision."

The Corporate Development Committee advises Business Objective managers of how much to expect for the coming year. While some shifts are possible, this advice generally prevents wasted effort on preparing detailed proposals vastly in excess of the possible strategic funding. This allocation is made on the basis of the Objectives' Planning Conference inputs. (The Annual Planning Conference is held in the Spring, usually in March.) Inputs include information on the business outlook, as the Objective managers define it, growth expectations, and present position, including current-year expenditures and milestone progress. The Strategy managers then rank Decision Packages, which prioritize tactical plans. These are turned over to Objective managers whose responsibility it is to rank-order these proposals for presentation to the Corporate Development Committee. The initial ranking is based on the preliminary allocation or budget suggested by the Corporate Development Committee. This represents a change over former procedure, as Charles Phipps, a corporate staff manager of Strategic Planning, noted:

> Our initial allocation is to give them a framework about how much money to expect. Up to about three years ago [that is, until 1972] we didn't do that, and we found people going through a needless exercise

FIGURE 5.4

Return on Assets (ROA)—History and Goals

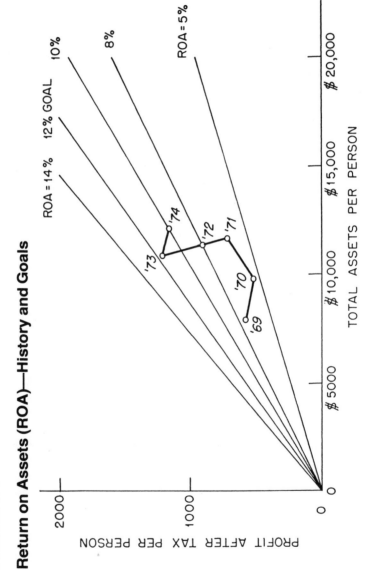

Source: Texas Instruments, Inc.

106

with their managers, where they would draw up plans to spend $20 million, when we could've told them, "We're thinking of only $6 to $8 million to give you next year." A good deal of frustration developed. So now we tell them.*

STANDARDIZING THE SYSTEM

In building in the OST, as in building in Taylor's procedures for oiling a machine or any other system, there are substantial advantages to a standardized format. With innovation as with any routine, without rules there cannot be exceptions, or management by exceptions. If the management of innovation was truly to be delegated, top-level management attention had to be abstracted from *doing* to *managing* and *coordinating*. In turn, this created the possibility of a much greater effective "span of control"—top management could delegate actual project management, and hence oversee many more projects. As the company grew, of course, more and more projects were needed.

In order to compress the information necessary to evaluate an OST Decision Package, the format of presentation has been standardized (see Figures 5.5, 5.6, 5.7, 5.8, and 5.9). As Phipps noted, the benefits of comparability, familiarity, and so on, are apparent.

Because we have to look at so many packages, we've standardized to have them put their Decision Package on foils. They can use as many back-up foils as they need to explain. But for comparison, this is what's called the Decision Package; why it's being done, what the approach is, what the goals are, in any units he cares to use; what is the status of the parameter at present, and what will be the status when the package is finished? It might be a cost goal, it might be a market penetration goal, it might be a product performance goal, or a combination of goals. What are the principal milestones, by event and date—he must have at least one per quarter—and responsibilities? What assumptions does he make on other packages: what does he assume might be running concurrently, or need to get started, that might be in a different package? What are the resources required, in terms of expense money, people, capital

---

*Personal Interview, 1975 series. Charles Phipps, a corporate staff manager of Strategic Planning, is a rarity at TI, where there are very few staff positions. Most staff jobs are rotated among operating personnel, who serve a brief stint usually as part of a seasoning procedure. Successful people, for whom the corporation has great expectations, are typically those chosen for staff jobs.

All quotations by Phipps, unless otherwise identified, refer to this interview series.

FIGURE 5.5

OST Decision Package, Form 1

OST DECISION PACKAGE SUMMARY

PACKAGE NAME		ORIGINATOR	DATE	OBJ	STGY	APPROVAL	DATE

STATEMENT OF NEED

MEASURABLE GOALS — INITIAL — COMPLETE

PRIMARY

SECONDARY

APPROACH

MILESTONES

EVENT — DATE — RESPONSIBILITY

OST RESOURCES	Last Year	1 Q	2 Q	3 Q	4 Q	Total	Next Year	MODEL IMPACT	197_	197_	197_	197_
Gross $								Δ's NSB $				
Net $												
E-People								Index No.				
N-F People								GPM				
Capital Exp.								Op Exp.				
								OST Exp.				

ASSUMPTIONS
Initiation/Parallel

Full Implementation

Source: Texas Instruments, Inc.

108

FIGURE 5.6

OST Decision Package, Form 2

STRATEGY NAME		STRATEGY NO.	
		PAGE OF	
MAJOR LONG RANGE CHECKPOINTS			
CHECKPOINTS	RESPONSIBILITY	DATE TO BEGIN	DATE TO COMPLETE

TI—9966

Source: Texas Instruments, Inc.

FIGURE 5.7

OST Decision Package, Form 3

STRATEGY NAME		STRATEGY NO.	
		PAGE	OF

CONTRIBUTION AND/OR POSSIBLE IMPACT

INCOME PRODUCING STRATEGIES:

	PREVIOUS YEAR	CURRENT YEAR	NEXT YEAR	FIFTH YEAR	TENTH YEAR
Net Sales Billed					
Division Profit					
Capital Requirements					
Success Probability					

PROFIT ENHANCING STRATEGIES:

	PREVIOUS YEAR	CURRENT YEAR	NEXT YEAR	FIFTH YEAR	TENTH YEAR
Cost Savings or Advoidance					
Expense					
Capital Requirements					
Success Probability					

ORGANIZATION SUPPORT STRATEGIES:

	PREVIOUS YEAR	CURRENT YEAR	NEXT YEAR	FIFTH YEAR	TENTH YEAR
Expense					
Capital Requirements					
Success Probability					

Source: Texas Instruments, Inc.

FIGURE 5.8

Tactical Action Program, Form 1

TACTICAL ACTION PROGRAM	PROGRAM NUMBER	OBJECTIVE	STRATEGY	DIVISION	TAP	PAGE OF
TI—10818						1

PROGRAM TITLE	STRATEGY TITLE

PROGRAM RESPONSIBILITY	START DATE	COMPLETE DATE	OBJECTIVE TITLE	STRATEGY RESPONSIBILITY

MAJOR QUANTITATIVE GOAL		
	OVER TAP LIFE	FROM / TO
	OVER PLAN YEAR	FROM / TO

STATEMENTS OF PROGRAM CONTRIBUTION

SUPPORT REQUIREMENTS		OVER TAP LIFE	OVER PLAN YEAR
	TOTAL PROFESSIONAL EFFORT - MAN MO'S		
	CAPITAL - $000		

ASSISTANCE REQUIRED FROM OTHER ORGANIZATIONS

ORGAN UNIT	APPROVAL	TYPE OF ASSISTANCE	INDIVIDUAL RESPONSIBLE	START DATE	COMPLETE DATE	PROFESS MAN-MO'S

PREPARED BY	DATE	APPROVED BY	DATE	REVISIONS
				1. 2. 3.

TACTICS PLANNED FOR PROGRAM COMPLETION	INDIVIDUAL RESPONSIBLE	START DATE	COMPLETE DATE	PROFESS. MAN-MO'S

Source: Texas Instruments, Inc.

FIGURE 5.9

Tactical Action Program, Form 2

TACTICAL ACTION PROGRAM TI–10817-B	PROGRAM NUMBER	OBJECTIVE	STRATEGY	DIVISION	TAP	PAGE OF
TACTICS PLANNED FOR PROGRAM COMPLETION			INDIVIDUAL RESPONSIBLE	START DATE	COMPLETE DATE	PROFESS MAN-MO'S

Source: Texas Instruments, Inc.

expenditures? If it's successful, what impact will it have on his financial model in some future year, either in terms of dollar billing or performance index change?

The standardized format, by offering guidance, created certain expectations of what is relevant. It encouraged managers to evaluate their projects in these terms, because the system does, and that's how money is to be allocated. These are the steps that must be completed and "Unless you do it that way, you're not going to get your money."

One intent of this pressure is to insure adequate monitoring of programs. This is a refinement over the original OST. As such, it emphasizes the seriousness of management attention to OST-related activities (and now, also, P&AE activities). It serves also to reinforce linkages with other facets of the management system, by providing another index to be taken into account in personnel evaluation. Charles Phipps described the change:

> For the first five years of OST implementation, plans were developed and action programs defined, but there was no control on the extent of resources being applied on a current basis. In order to close the loop and control the resources actually being applied to strategic programs, all expenses were divided into either operating or strategic funds. . . . Strategic expenses are collected by project; and, further, they are itemized as a separate line item on each Department [PCC] Profit and Loss Statement.[1]

The monitoring here, as in Operations, is on an exception basis, to control expenditures, finances, and reporting of results. What is reported and considered are measures or indexes, not details. In addition, Phipps commented, the monitoring of control indexes goes beyond earlier practice, which was a review once or twice a year. Current practice is to examine milestone progress, as well as dollar expenditures.

> We watch this, in a down year, to make sure he's spending it. And we monitor the milestones to make sure the funds are being spent on the right milestones. If the manager underspends in this area, he's in just as much trouble as if he overspends. . . . This gives us an overview of the PCCs.

Both aspects of the interface between strategic activities and operating activities are visible here: operating people are involved, and top management is most interested in strategic matters. While strategic expenses are separated from operating expenses and ultimately collected on a project basis, they occur in fact within the PCC. Thus they appear "below the line," as segregated strategic expenditures on a PCC profit and loss statement, as well. (Figure 4.4 illustrates this format.) Line managers, people with operating responsibilities, carry out the strategic programs of the corporation in tandem with on-going business. As Haggerty pointed out, "It's a principle of the system that it is done by those people who are responsible for the success of the organization—not by a bunch of staff people."

The function of the OST in directing top-level attention is equally apparent, as Haggerty went on to note. "We *insist* on the top people themselves being involved in it—this is the way it's worked from the beginning. It is a way of organizing *their* time with respect to the future."

The top-to-bottom, bottom-to-top involvement is equally visible in the planning procedure as described by Charles Phipps:

> Our planning at TI takes place in what we call four loops, building up from the bottom. Each department or PCC Manager makes a forecast every month, for the next four months, and that is considered a profit commitment by the Corporation that he's expected to make, with few excuses. Once a quarter—building up from this—they will project their businesses for the next six to eight quarters out, on a rolling basis. We use this now, instead of an annual plan. This becomes the financial plan, and the variances are made against this, and performance is measured against this.
>
> At the Strategic Planning Conference, we focus on these two: the intermediate range plan, for the next three years; and the long-range growth plan, for the next five or ten years. From the intermediate plan are determined what we call Model of the Year Parameters, or Performance Indexes, for each of the PCCs, for the next three years. So we can look out and see where he must improve himself in order to attain his Model of the Year Performance Measures for at least three years. The Long Range Plan is for five and ten year growth.

As described above, all of this filters up eventually as high as the Board of Directors, with top-level consideration and familiarity fairly early on in the Development Committee and in Strategic Planning sessions (both preliminary sessions and the full-dress, week long conference).

MONITORING INNOVATION: BY NEGOTIATION

Monitoring innovation—by definition not specifiable in advance—is critical to controlling it. Thus, the milestones each quarter are fundamental to the working of the OST. These indicators, which are suggested by the writer of the Decision Package, usually the Strategy Manager, can be in any measurable parameter suitable to the project undertaken. However, the indicators must be definite and discrete, to provide for adequate monitoring of progress. Phipps and Don Spalinger* gave some examples:

Spalinger:
   They are things you can really affix a date to: you know, say that "It was accomplished on this date," not "Well, yeah, we kinda did that last week."
Phipps:
   If it's a design product, it might be initial requirements defined, worked out with marketing assessments, that these really are going to be the requirements. You may have a feasibility model of a certain section . . . there's one section [of a project] where technically, you're not sure whether you can do it. So you'd like to find out—for this section, the milestone might be, "Prove feasibility by a certain date." There may be some long-lead tooling items, so, "Release long-lead tooling items by a certain date." You may be asked to go through certain reliability or qualification tests: you'll start tests on a certain date, and complete tests. Or "Release manufacturing tooling," "Start pilot line operation," realize a certain level of performance, and so on.

The assembled Decision Packages (with goals, milestones, and the names of those responsible, resource requirements, and any significant interconnections with other programs) are prioritized. The Objective manager ranks them, down to the cut-off line of anticipated OST funds. There is room for negotiation. In addition, the Objective manager will "show half a dozen or so *below* the cut-off line in order to get additional monies," according to Phipps. These programs are by no means out of the question, even though they exceed the forecast of available OST funds for a given Objective. The Corporate Development Committee reviews each Objective's Decision Packages, challenging them and, if appropriate, shifting funds among Objectives:

   Some Objectives will come in surprises, with a stronger program than we thought they could have, and we may give them more money. People who are in a strong growth position may really have pretty weak programs. We may cut back and tell them, "Well, all right, we said six million, this is only worth four and a half. You go back and rework this program, and we'll look at in in March." We'll only fund it for one quarter.

Some project money is held back as unallocated funds, reserved for projects not presented at this time, or for new businesses which might occur during the year. Of particular interest to the Corporate Development

---

*Personal Interview, 1975 series. At the time of the interview Don Spalinger was on the corporate Strategic Planning Staff.

Committee in this regard are proposals which "really don't belong in the current Business Objectives." Project proposals associated with a current Business Objective which fall "below the line" are termed the "Creative Backlog." Perhaps some half or two-thirds of the Decision Packages presented by the Strategy Manager to the Objective Manager involve continuing programs. These are usually funded only on a one-year basis. Typically, the Strategy Manager must decide, on the basis of progress and available alternatives, which programs to propose for funding and which to cut. (The Strategy manager may or may not receive guidance from the Objective manager.) In the event of unexpected progress, the Strategy manager may seek to generate additional funding for existing programs, or he may also seek funding for new programs. Progress in relation to milestones, not cost-cutting, is the criterion. The impact of a strategy program may well warrant additional effort, rather than a "savings" effort or an efficiency focus.

In negotiations with the Corporate Development Committee, several interactions may occur in the ranking process. Initially, the Objective Managers use the criteria that appear best to them in prioritizing their programs. In keeping with its corporate-level focus and coordinating duties, the Corporate Development Committee will pay attention to balance among functional areas. Frequently the Objective Manager will anticipate this.

> To make sure that he's covering his areas, he may make functional rankings—in other words, go through all these and take all the marketing packages and rank them separately, just on marketing. Take all the design packages, rank those; take all the process support, and rank those; and so forth, and do a functional ranking. It's interesting to see how well you've covered in your functional areas. Even though you're not organized functionally, you'll see if you're maintaining your functional strengths, or do you have enough resources in some of these areas.
>
> So they'll use three or four different methods—each one has his own style of arriving at some ranking to satisfy himself that this is the best mix of strategic effort that he can pursue, with the amount of funds that he has.

This ranked list is presented to the Corporate Development Committee. The Objective Manager presents his rationale for selection along with the list, and negotiations ensue. As Len Donohoe, himself a strategy manager, put it:*

---

*Personal Interview, 1975 series. At the time of the interview Donohoe was Strategy Manager for the Scientific Calculator business, and Operations Manager for much of the calculator engineering effort.

At different operational levels, conflicts are resolved in different ways, usually with a lot of top-down direction as to what priorities are. But we do prioritize in rank order all the time, at all levels. Then we review that, with the Corporate OST [Development] Committee. . . . One of the beauties of the OST System is that, if you do it properly, you've identified twice as many programs as you can hope to fund. This results in disappointment, *tremendous* disappointment on the part of individual contributors, people that have put good programs together that fall below the line. That's one of the necessary evils of the system, if you want to refer to it as an evil. But you come up with a rank ordering. A lot of people don't want to do this; they want to rank several of them number one. But under the proper discipline, you've just got to apply a rank order. This relates to a budget, and programs are selected to match funds available. Very often, at a departmental level, you'll find that programs selected will be rather short-sighted programs. They're the next year, year-and-a-half type programs, rather than long-term. And sure enough, just below that line is your wild hare—the thing that has a big risk, but if you succeed, there's a big gain. It comes below that line: it's a part of the game that gets played, between operations and corporate people.

Donohoe then recounted the negotiations procedure:

Now, the gentlemen that sit over there in the North Building on the OST Committee are very forward-thinking men—that's how they got where they are. They're really awfully interested in *that* program because of the thrust of the Corporation. So here it is, below the line. When you go over there with that kind of a ranking, very often they'll say, "Uh-uh. Your rankings are wrong. *That's* number one." Now, it is your job to figure out how to achieve your results within these constraints, since that's the reason you're a manager, to solve that kind of problem.

So very often after a review by the OST Committee, you march out of there with a different rank ordering. Then it's in the hands of the operations people.

The Corporate Development Committee, in its consideration, pays particular attention to the bottom line:

We look particularly at the bottom line—the 10 or 20 percent of the [Decision] Packages immediately above and those immediately below the bottom line. We'll really look at these in some detail, as to whether the ones above are really worth while, or should we cut them out—or are any of the ones below worthwhile, that we should bring up. We'll do a cross-comparison with Operating Packages [non-strategic current-year plans] which were ranked for another committee—we'll ask to see

them, to see whether there should be any cross-shifting. There are a
series of things we do.

It is apparent here that, if the Operating managers are playing a game with
the corporate people, as Donohoe suggests, it is recognized and matched
by counter-moves.*

Counter-moves by the Corporate Development Committee include
specifiic direction. An Objective's emphasis and thrust may be revised on
the basis of the view from the top.

> There's a letter from the Chairman of the OST Committee which
> follows in a day or two of the review, recommending specific action.
> Here's a copy of a letter which went out after an Objective review of the
> electrical controls business. They didn't like this strategy at all, and
> they did recommend this shift . . . to another recommendation that went
> out to the semiconductor folks after a review of their 1973 plans. We
> were concerned that they didn't have enough money in one area, and
> we felt that it should be increased by $353,000. We also felt they could
> cut back on the highspeed logic area. To do that—to cut back—we told
> them where they could get their money. "You're spending too much
> money in the small signal area, you should be spending in the power
> area." The OST Committee didn't like their programs, so we funded
> only for a quarter—"You can come back to try to get the rest."

Another change has been a concerted effort to require more comprehensive decision packages. Particularly since 1972–73, the Corporate Development Committee has sought to eliminate a practice of breaking a program
into many small decision packages "in order to get half or three-quarters of
it funded, rather than playing 'all or nothing' with us," as Phipps described
it. This, countermove, in conjunction with a growth in the dollar size and
complexity of the projects the company could afford to be interested in, has
kept TAPs at between 250 and 300 during the 1970s. The number of TAPs
has not grown in proportion to increases in OST funding.

Strong direction—subject to negotiation and discussion, and based on
inputs from below—is inevitable in a system designed to raise strategic
activities into high visibility. Top-level involvement and intervention of
this nature is appropriate. The size of strategic expenditures and their
impact upon the future of the firm are substantial. The decisions thus
acquire a character of "futurity" and "irreversibility" in Peter Drucker's
terms.[2]

---

*The reader is referred to G.H. Hofstede, *The Game of Budget Control*, for a discussion
of the functional aspects of this outlook for budgetary control (London: Tavistock, 1968).

PEOPLE AND ASSET EFFECTIVENESS:
AN ITERATION OF THE OST

Once the OST was reasonably well built into the system of management at Texas Instruments, the final step in institutionalizing it could be taken; the knowledge and procedures which the OST applied to technical innovation could be generalized. This generalization is both the cause and effect of institutionalization. Until the OST was fairly well institutionalized, it could not be generalized; but once it was generalized, it permeated the entire management structure of the company, and was well and truly institutionalized.

The People and Asset Effectiveness program is a resource-utilization effort modelled after the OST. Like the OST, the P&AE is a top-to-bottom effort. Like it too, the P&AE functions as a series of hierarchically-linked goals supported by goal-directed action plans. Line managers plan and implement the P&AE activities, in addition to their operating responsibilities, again like the OST. Programs are explicitly intended for application across the corporation—a conscious effort at the same kind of synergy the OST is intended to provide in strategic activities. And expenses here, as with the OST, are aggregated separately from operating expenses. TI feels that growth-related OST activities and the P&AE program reinforce one another.

> As the effectivity [sic] of our resources improved, through productivity gains, better utilization of resources or more involvement in problem-solving by our people, our growth programs are impacted through the availability of more funds for investment or improved solutions to our customer's requirements.[3]

The synergistic impact of OST methodology is perhaps more visible in P&AE programs than in technological innovation. Improved materials handling or a more effective training program is more apparently transferable than technical efforts—even in a company that seeks to develop technical ideas beyond the obvious applications. Like the more technological OST programs, P&AE programs are proposal-based, project-oriented efforts. They are not required for the attainment of current-year financial or production forecasts (and therefore, in TI terminology, they are "discretionary"). And they are formulated around specific goals, explicit directions, definite beginnings and endpoints, and specified milestones en route.

P&AE programs concern the more effective development of people, the more efficient use of assets, employee benefit packages, personnel development, as well as information and design systems, materials handling, and productivity. Here is the OST methodology in its essence: goal-

FIGURE 5.10

Average Percentage Change per Year

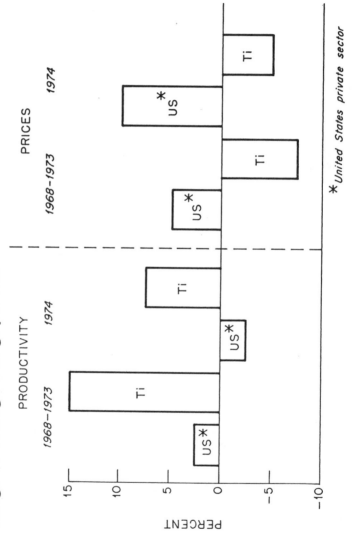

Source: Texas Instruments, Inc.

FIGURE 5.11

Management Planning and Control at Texas Instruments

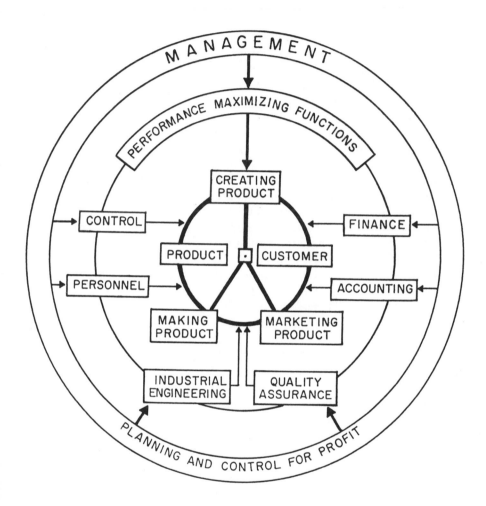

Source: Texas Instruments, Inc.

directed activities, the hierarchy of goals supported by short-range implementation plans, projects specified in endpoints and milestones, top-level attention and all-level involvement. It is adapted to spreading already-discovered improvements for use throughout the corporation.

P&AE is the most recent of TI's management systems. Like its sisters, the OST and PCC systems, P&AE is a corporation-wide, top-to-bottom network of information, programmatic activity, and, importantly, of funding. The funding and the top-level attention, as with the OST system, serve here to underline the seriousness of management intentions, reinforcing the perception that "these programs matter." Familiarity with mechanisms, based on the already-institutionalized OST, helped to generalize the P&AE.

Like the OST and PCC structures, the P&AE System grew out of a desire to institutionalize top-management interests. Both Haggerty and his successor as President, Mark Shepherd, Jr., had for some years been concerned with increasing productivity. TI's annual reports since 1971 have given space to the company's productivity efforts, including training programs, work-simplification efforts, and substantial capital investments in programs like computer-assisted circuit design. One of TI's assumptions, identical to that prevalent in the U.S. machine-tool industry of the late 1800s, incidentally, is that capital investment in special-purpose equipment, with the consequent pressure for higher quantities and lower prices, is essential to success. This assumption is readily apparent in TI's productivity measures. TI measures productivity as a percentage return on assets per person employed. The corporation sets goals here, as in growth-related activities. Managers are assigned responsibility for P&AE Objectives, Strategies and TAPs, which are based on proposals submitted in roughly the same format as OST Decision Packages. Thus goals for the late 1970s were a Return on Assets of $1,500 to $1,800 on assets of $15,000 per employee (see Figure 5.4). Increasing investment is seen as a productivity-maximizing strategy, a way to compete with the lower labor costs of less-developed countries by building new knowledge permanently into each employee's job. Investment in automated circuit design and manufacturing capabilities are examples. They allow substantial reductions in materials costs as well as increases in output per worker (see Figures 5.10 and 5.11), resulting in lower per-unit costs.

P&AE measurement at Texas Instruments dates from about 1969—when, according to Haggerty, the OST was "really in"—although productivity improvement efforts and the effective use of all resources (explicitly including people) have long been company goals. For instance, to encourage development of general management skills, TI managers typically have been given early responsibilities. One of the stated aims of the OST System, for instance (and here again the interconnection between various aspects of the TI management systems becomes visible), is to broaden the general managerial base by pushing short-term/long-term trade-offs and strategic thinking farther down into the organization. Similarly, the PCCs' design of "many little businesses" is aimed quite specifically at developing a marketing viewpoint and a sense of balance at the lowest possible level, where managers are in daily contact with the reality facing the company, and where they can be expected to respond more quickly. On a still lower level, Work Simplification Training programs have included production people from their early days. Operators' input is encouraged in the form of specific suggestions on how to simplify their jobs. As with the OST, the involvement of people at all levels in the P&AE System serves to institutionalize it, and serves as well to reinforce both ownership of the programs, and the shared frame of reference they create.

As with the OST System, to indicate management's seriousness about the program, top corporate officers announced the People and Asset Effectiveness thrust and its results. In 1971, at the annual stockholders' meeting, TI president Mark Shepherd, Jr. announced the program. He noted that the expected results were related to operating results as well as human relations.

> People and Assets Effectiveness is an improved ability to solve customers' problems through increased productivity of people and assets. It means improved planning and control systems. It means the application of automation to design, to manufacturing, and to management problems. And, most importantly, it means the fullest use of all the talents of each TIer. This requires opportunities for TIers to use their minds as well as their hands—to be involved in the planning and control of their work, not simply the doing. . . .[4]

Two years later, Shepherd emphasized the impact of productivity increases on TI's prices.

> Over the 1960–71 time period, TI has not only far outdistanced average productivity increases for the United States and Germany, but also has more than kept pace with Japan, the recognized productivity leader. This high rate of improvement was continued during 1972 and, as a direct result of this productivity record, average prices for TI products and services were decreased for the tenth consecutive year. This is a record matched by few organizations anywhere in the world. . . .*

---

*Mark Shepherd, Jr., Presentation to the annual stockholders' meeting, 1973. For an intriguing extended discussion of some related issues from a public viewpoint, the reader is referred to *The Human Economic* by Eli Ginzberg (New York: McGraw-Hill, 1976).

Conspicuous modelling on the OST System, and conspicuous signals of top-level interest in the program were quick to appear. The company chose to implement the P&AE program with a corporate-level committee, operating in tandem with the old OST Committee (which was renamed first the Growth Committee, then the Corporate Development Committee). In 1975, the P&AE Committee was headed by executive vice-president A. Ray McCord. (Later, the P&AE activities were transferred to the Corporate Development Committee.) In a similar fashion the people responsible for the programs at lower levels were also experienced line people, not staff personnel. Chuck Anders, the corporate manager for P&AE, came to the job after heading TI's Asian Semiconductor Manufacturing operations. He had some 17 years in production and marketing, and described himself as "a P&L man." As with the original OST System, the calibre of those appointed to positions of responsibility created expectations of success— individual success, on the basis of track record, and system success, by virtue of the individual's ability to make things happen. This practice facilitates the development of legitimacy and importance for the new activity. The idea is, "Make those who'll *implement* the plans *make* the plans."[5] Anders described the working of the P&AE activities within the system as supplementing the OST activities, and very much modelled on OST experiences and aims:

> The company is run by an Operating Committee—always has been. The Operating Committee divides the funds available to it [for strategic purposes] between the OST Committee and the P&AE Committee. . . . They spend money within each one of their Business Objectives on People and Asset Effectiveness Programs that are unique to their own Business Objective. The P&AE Committee spends money on programs that . . . can be fanned out across all Business Objectives, such as energy conservation programs, or management information systems programs, . . . or manufacturing automation programs that could be used by every Business Objective across the corporation.
>
> So the OST people are taking care of their new products, and their individual market segments and market share, providing for the innovations that they need to improve productivity of their people and assets in their own business. Then all of the businesses of the corporation are being supported by funds on specific programs such as these that are horizontal in nature: not vertical, just within the Business, but across the entire corporation.*

---

*Personal Interview, 1975 series. Willis H. "Chuck" Anders, III, was Corporate Manager of People and Asset Effectiveness at the time of the interview. Anders' recent experience included heading TI's Asian semiconductor manufacturing facilities, a line operations slot.

The P&AE programs are funded through a process of selection much like that for OST Programs for growth. Indeed, the differences are in content, rather than method, as Anders noted.

> We have Intercompany Objectives, and we use the OST System in managing these activities, just as we do for growth. We have an Intercompany Objective for our manufacturing automation programs. We have Strategies and Tactical Action Programs underneath that particular Intercompany Objective. Combined with that, as it happens, is a design automation program. This is a management system for information—actually for simplification: we call it Information Systems and Services Intercompany Objective. There's a Facilities Effectiveness program, which includes our energy conservation; there's a Material Effectiveness, and one we call Liquidity—that handles cash, receivables and inventory. Then there's a People Effectiveness ICO that takes care of involvement programs, affirmative action or EEO programs, employee development, and Success Sharing, all of the benefit-type programs for the people. So you can see, I think, that these types of programs—or when we talk about material effectiveness, which has to do with the automation of warehousing, or the information systems for purchasing and receiving, and for carrying accounts payable or accounts reveivable and so forth—all of those things could be applicable to any Business we have, across the corporation.

Both Phipps and Haggerty had also alluded to the OST methods as promoting synergy. Phipps stressed technological innovation:

> The third characteristic of the OST system is the synergistic impact gained by coupling the capabilities of different businesses. We strongly believe that the technology developed in one business can often be concurrently coupled with that of other businesses so that the Corporation realizes something more than the individual sums of the standalone businesses. The OST system provides the means to couple activities that otherwise would have minimal interaction.[6]

Synergies of innovation are explicitly more than "hard technology" alone, as Haggerty emphasized from the beginning:

> I must make clear the breadth of innovation we have in mind. . . . The fact is that critical innovation may occur in the *make* and *market* functions as well as in the *create* function. Further, the effective innovation is the integral of the innovation in all three of the categories: create, make, and market. . . .[7]

Anders described the evolution of a formal P&AE thrust as the application of OST methods: explicit goals and responsibility, corporation-wide application, and, by implication, line management implementation.

Until last Fall [1974] we only had vertical-type of P&AE programs . . . as such. We had horizontal programs, but they weren't P&AE. . . . The reason they really weren't P&AE was that they didn't have anybody responsible for them, outside of the Business Objective. These Business Objectives each have a P&AE Strategy, and they have a Strategy Manager within each one of these businesses. He manages a group of funds that may represent 25 percent of the total funds that are put into that particular Business Objective—but it's unique to it. And we've done a real good job of that; we've done a good job of this business, and so forth. Where we haven't done a good job is that this program that is put into this Business Objective may be also applicable to that Business Objective, and this Business Objective. And we haven't fanned those out. Now what we've done is we've taken the key people within the Corporation, the people that manage these Intercompany Objectives, and they're Committee members—our key people from each one of these Business Objectives. So now we have a structured organization, if you will, that gives us representation from across the Corporation, working on, say material effectiveness.

Anders went on to make the line-management orientation more specific, and to explain the reasoning behind it.

We don't have, and I don't believe we ever will have, a Corporate Materials Manager . . . because the businesses are still unique. But I believe that we'll continue to have a Corporate Material Effeceveness Intercompany Objective that will have the materials managers, procurement and materials managers, from each one of these Business Objectives, active on it. . . . We've got the ability to have 10 or 12 managers responsible for the corporate material, rather than just one. And it's another way also that we have of achieving another corporate objective, manager development. We feel very strongly that one of our shortcomings, five to ten years from now, is going to be the availability of managerial personnel. By having these types of Intercompany Objectives, that are managed by people from across the corporation that are at a lower level than our Business Objective managers, we have the opportunity to develop 12 times as many managerial personnel for our future growth and development as we would if we had just one doing it. . . . It's a good opportunity for us to achieve a couple of things—to fan out these activities across the corporation, and also to develop for our future managerial needs. . . . With more people involved in managing the corporation, a few people don't have to make arbitrary decisions.

To integrate the P&AE activities with on-going business, TI has generalized the OST methodology. Anders noted that evaluation of P&AE performance is on the basis of

quantified goals. Each ICO—there are eight of them—each has an Objective Statement, some Strategic guidelines, and some *measures.*

. . . It's structured just like the OST system. Those measures are quantified, and they have long-term and intermediate-type goals.

The impact of the P&AE is twofold: on the one hand, it represents a new thrust of managerial activity and attention—toward efficient resource utilization. On the other,the P&AE activities represent a further step in the institutionalization of the OST and its methodology throughout the Texas Instruments management system. In the P&AE System, both the original characteristics of the OST (specific long-range goals; hierarchical linkages between these Objectives, the intermediate range Strategies and the short-run Tactics to implement them) and the later refinements (specific managerial responsibility, explicit milestones, segregated expenditures, corporation-wide applicability, and management development aims) were adapted to non-technological, not necessarily innovative programs. By providing an iteration of the OST methodology—generalizing it to management practice rather than leaving it as a discrete innovation and technical activity—the P&AE furthers the process of OST institutionalization even as it gives evidence of it.

SUMMARY

Management systems at Texas Instruments have evolved, step by step, as experience was accumulated or better ways discovered. The original system, the PCC, grew out of the product line diversification *conceptualized* as far back as 1948 or 1949, but only *realized*—in decentralized, product-line reorganization—in 1954. The formal, organizational institutionalization of reorganization builds into the administrative system, into the organization, the conceptual insight shared by only a few managers in earlier days. Thoughtful reflection by top management, notably by Patrick Haggerty and his close associates, devised the OST System to provide a parallel crystallization of their insights in project management to the administrative systems of the corporation as a whole. As time went on, other managers revised the OST system. The OST was a consciously designed, consciously evolved means to institutionalize the forward planning and strategic thinking which had rested with these few top managers until the early 1960s. Growth, the need for more and larger projects, and a consciousness of the need to coordinate *many* projects aimed at innovation (in order to direct them, and to steer the company as a whole toward a planned future) were the spurs to the evolution of the OST System. In developing the OST, an explicit parallel was drawn between product-line decentralization and the decentralization of strategic thinking. In a similar fashion, attention to productivity and resource utilization (including people) led to the People and Assets Effectiveness program, again explicitly modelled on past successes, this time the OST. Here, the OST's methodology was generalized and applied to another class of projects.

APPENDIX

Managers Interviewed at Texas Instruments

Willis "Chuck" Anders — Corporate Manager for People and Asset Effectiveness. Formerly in charge of Asian Semiconductor Manufacturing. Wide and varied operations experience; currently staff.

Don Brooks — PCC Manager for linear integrated circuits, as well as Strategy Manager for the same area.

Phil Coup — Assistant Objective Manager for the Electronic Function Objective, Semiconductor Business. He was also Strategy Manager for the Discrete Devices (transistors) area. At the time of the interview, in a staff position with no direct operating responsibility.

Harvey Cragon — Strategy Manager for microprocessors. Was Strategy Manager for the Advanced Scientific Computer effort for a number of years (this was a major TI development effort).

Len Donohoe — Strategy Manager for Scientific Calculators. Operating Manager for much of the calculator engineering effort as well.

Ralph Dosher — Assistant Objective Manager for Calculator Products. Formerly head of Strategic Planning during the formative stages of the OST's development, during the late 1960s. Operations Manager for Appliance Control area prior to Charles Flanagan.

Norman Einspruch — Assistant Vice President for Corporate Development.

Charles Flanagan — Strategy Manager for Appliance Controls, as well as PCC manager for this area; both strategic and operating responsibilities.

Patrick Haggerty — Retired former president and chief executive officer, and chairman of the Board of TI. Prime architect of the OST and TI's other management systems.

Turner Hasty — Director of the Semiconductor Research and Development Laboratory. Formerly at the Central Research Laboratory.

Gene Helms — Laboratory head for the Systems and Information Sciences Laboratory section of the Central Research Laboratory. Formerly head of Strategic Planning.

Bill Kennedy — Staff Assistant to Strategy Manager for Business Information Systems and Services.

Russ Logan — Strategy Manager and PCC Operations Manager for Radar Systems in the Equipment Group.

Paul Maycock — Leaving TI to go to ERDA to pursue an interest in developing solar energy. "Super staff"—recently in charge of product research and market research in Consumer Products.

Mike Nevaris — P&AE Strategy Manager for the Government Electronics Objectives. Operations management responsibility for Quality and Reliability Assurance for the Equipment Group.

Charles Phipps — Manager, Corporate Strategy. A staff position.

Judy Roberts — Corporate Development Staff.

Bill Schneider — Assistant Objective Manager in the Services Group. He has operating responsibility for most of the engineering effort as well.

William Sick — Assistant Vice President on special assignment as a "super" Objective Manager for the Industrial Activity. He was in charge of Corporate Development during 1974–75. His background includes operations management responsibilities in semiconductors. At the time of the interview, he had no operating responsibilities.

Dean Toombs — Objective Manager for the Electronic Function Objective, and Operational responsibility for major technology development effort in semiconductors.

Cam Wason — Program Manager for some new seismic processing techniques in the Service Business.

Bud Whitney — Strategy Manager for Management Information Systems.

NOTES

1. "The OST System: A Management Approach to the Realization of Growth and Resource Goals." A presentation to the Corporate Growth Association, St. Louis, Mo., Sept. 9, 1975, by Charles H. Phipps, Corporate Development, Texas Instruments, Inc. Photo offset, pages not numbered.

2. Peter F. Drucker, *The Practice of Management* (New York: Harper, 1954).

3. Phipps, "The OST System."

4. Mark Shepherd, Jr., Presentation to the annual stockholders' meeting, 1971.

5. Patrick E. Haggerty, informal address at the Graduate School of Business, Hrvard University, March 1975. Personal transcript notes.

6. Phipps, "The OST System."

7. Patrick Haggerty, "Management Philosophies and Practices." A Presentation at Texas Instruments Annual Planning Conference, Dec., 1964. In *Management Philosophies and Practices of Texas Instruments, Incorporated*. Published in 1965 by Texas Instruments, Inc., Dallas, Texas.

INSTITUTIONALIZING INNOVATION:

SOME THEORETICAL SPECULATIONS

A brief survey of some developments in management practice, from the beginnings of systematic management by Taylor and Church through the complex administrative systems of Du Pont, General Motors and Texas Instruments, reveals some interesting patterns and progressions. All of the administrative systems surveyed have one critical characteristic in common: they stipulate a way of thinking about and responding to a class of situations. The systems deal with progressively more complex, abstract, and generalized situations. At the lower end of this spectrum, the focus is upon replication of concrete, specific actions. Once this is achieved, however, more inclusive coordination becomes possible; and, rather than specifying the *content*, higher-level systems focus upon *process*. At the higher end of the spectrum, it is suggested, the systems constitute rules for impounding new responses, for assessing and analyzing new situations. In this, they are qualitatively different from lower-level systems, which codify specific actions or limited ranges of response to pre-defined situations. True higher-level learning systems seek to institutionalize the means of change, maintaining and enhancing the organization's facility to acquire and preserve knowledge.

6/
LEARNING
IN ORGANIZATIONS

A BRIEF RETROSPECT

At this point, a retrospect seems in order, to draw together the varied threads of this study. Taylor and the early systematic management theorists confronted a plethora of detail. In the machine tool industry of the 1890s especially, increasing complexity and specialization required more managers, and thus more coordination among them to coordinate the firm as a whole. High-volume production made difficulties still more extreme. The problems were overwhelmingly managerial, rather than technical. What was needed was some systematic procedure for coordinating and monitoring, and, not inconsequentially, for abstracting the task of management from the details of job performance. Until an appropriate level of abstraction was defined, the problems of coordination were insoluble. In both the performance and the management of routine jobs, some means of transcending the particular individual was necessary. Until this means was found, industrial complexity was limited to what the individual could comprehend, remember, organize, perform, or control. The possibilities for organizational synergy were thereby similarly limited. Organizations needed methods of impounding and retaining the insights of individuals. Some means of replicating acceptable procedures persistently, predictably, and independently of the original discoverers, was necessary.

Systematic management techniques, from Taylor's excruciatingly detailed instructions on oiling a machine to Church's accounting systems, were the means to these ends. Taylor sought explicitly to record and codify in order to render the organization less dependent on the memory, good will, or physical presence of any particular employee. Equally, he sought to avoid the necessity of repeated rediscovery of efficient procedures by each worker. Just such a codification of concrete details of task performance is a reasonable description of one sort of "organizational memory." Withou resorting to reification, it is apparent that such a mechanism retains the knowledge of how to perform the task. Perhaps more important still, such a recording makes the knowledge accessible to others beyond the origina discoverer, eliminating the need to rediscover. Since the task is specified. the recording permits supervision of the task to proceed on a different level, by exceptions. Instructions create expectations and demands: *this* is the way to do it, not some other way; do *this*, don't spend time experimenting to possibly, fortuitously discover the proper way. Within limits, written instructions create a shared frame of reference and a shared experience—albeit vicarious, for others than the discoverer—of a proper way to accomplish the task.

Once the task itself is specified and can be replicated, managerial attention can shift to a different level of abstraction, treating this particular task and its performance as "given." On one level, this kind of simple replicability is evidence of organizational learning. Successful actions or behaviors can be specified and thus reiterated over time. This is the lower-level, routine learning that March and Simon[1] or Cyert and March[2] were willing to admit: a stored repertoire of successful sequences of action. By permitting the organization to transcend the particular discoverer of the knowledge, and by making it accessible to others, such programs allow for the synergy (on a rudimentary level at least) that I identified earlier as characteristic of organizations. The program or instructions specify required actions and, implicitly, the means of their coordination. Managerial attention can be freed from the need to coordinate here, and can look instead to coordinating among such sets of specified behaviors. These lower-level learning programs are so commonplace and pervasive that we frequently dismiss them as trivial, or ignore them altogether. However, they are the essential foundation for the development of higher-level systems. The lower-level programs create a means of synergy, the shared frame of reference which preserves knowledge. They also create a way of retaining and communicating learning beyond the individual who discovers it, making possible further refinement and more inclusive coordination. And, not incidentally, they substantially improve performance by eliminating the need to rediscover every time what has been learned before. This was Taylor's insight.

Taylor's contributions went beyond the simple recording of procedure, however. In his distinction between planning and performance, he built upon the codification of routine tasks and for the first time made possible the large-scale coordination of details—planning and policy-level thinking, above and beyond the details of the task itself. The initial steps are critical; without them, the manager and the organization remain inundated in details of the task, and abstraction is impossible for sheer want of information-processing capacity. This should not obscure the qualitative difference between the details of the task, and a focus on coordination of them. Taylor tended to focus on the coordination of the tasks of a single workman, or on the relationship among tasks in a single workflow at most. Nevertheless, instructions on how to coordinate such a group of activities is a step higher, a logical level above the elements themselves. To confuse the two is an error in logical typing, equivalent to confusing the map with the territory, the name with the thing, the recipe with the meal. Thus the "specialty" of records clerks who generate instructions is not the task itself, but a body of knowledge *about* many tasks. The frame of reference of the clerk transcends the frame of reference of any individual worker whose task is specified. Conceptually, this represents a clear shift to a level of logical abstraction superior to that of the task itself—that is, a more inclusive level. The clerk's perspective includes many tasks, and the technology for codifying them. In generating new sets of instructions, for instance, such questions as, "Does the sequence of actions performed by this worker mesh smoothly with others' actions?" and "Should Worker A notify Worker C when A's task is complete?" illustrate the logical distinction between the level of the task, and thinking *about* its specification. Another way of drawing the distinction is to note that the clerk's task includes specifying boundary-spanning communications or interfaces which relate self-contained segments; any individual worker need be concerned only with activities within the specification.

The division of labor, specialization, and subdivision of the task, encouraging detailed knowledge of a portion of the task in the individual worker, necessarily splits off coordination from performance. This is differentiation by another name. The reintegration necessary for efficient performance is provided by a higher frame of reference, that is, one inclusive enough to contain all the specialized elements. Taylor's methodology provided the means of implementing the specialized knowledge he disvered, of coordinating it, monitoring it, and assuring that performance was adequate. By specifying the details, management could insure replication of the best practices on the shop floor. By setting up roles and standards, management could be abstracted because the knowledge embodied in standards was accessible to the worker. Since the knowledge was accessible, its ordinary application could be delegated and management could concentrate on exceptions. The procedures and rules for relating various tasks—rudimentary codification of the management task—insured that here too, certain patterns were replicated, independent of their fortuitous rediscovery by each individual. It was no longer necessary to rediscover a right way; one had already been specified. This left management free to concentrate on exceptions, coordination, and new tasks. The details of management were specified; some were delegated (to functional foremen; although Taylor's system was never fully implemented successfully, many of the same tasks are separated into different staff jobs today); and a shared frame of reference was specified, guiding performance, perception and interpretation.

Church's further development of thinking about the management task generalized the insights that Taylor had applied to technical details. The accounting methods Church developed provided the means for abstracting management by making possible the description and monitoring of performance in diverse areas or products. The focus is upon how the details of the management task itself fit together; and, on a lower level, how the details of the managed task fit together. The "five great organic functions" of managerial work that Church identified are abstractions *about* the task of management, approaches to organizing the performance of tasks.

SYSTEMS FOR PLANNING, SYSTEMS FOR THOUGHT

General Motors and Du Pont offer higher-level analogues to the split Taylor proposed between the performance of a task and its planning and coordination. While there are clearly limits to the usefulness of the distinction,* nevertheless it is critical to the management of complex activities, especially when they are combined (as in the modern complex organization of diverse task specialties, products, or areas). Taylor's schemata systematized task details, focused management on coordination, and, by abstraction, freed up management to undertake the overarching tasks of planning and policy. In an analogous fashion, the extensive and sophisticated control systems of General Motors and Du Pont made feasible decentralized management in a complex organization. They thereby also made possible for the first time concerted coordination (that is, synergy) and true policy for such organizations. So long as management is overwhelmed by the details of task performance, planning and policy will not occur. March and Simon describe this phenomenon, a Gresham's Law of Planning: routine activities drive out long-range, nonroutine activities.[3] In this context, the absence of long-range planning "that makes a difference" is comprehensible, and with it the purely *re*active stance of organizations Cyert and March found. That is, until what is routine is systematized and

---

*The present-day interest in job-enrichment and participation can be seen as the result of too extensive a split between planning and performance, with dysfunctional consequences of alienation, loss of effective interface between the worker and the work, and so on. See "Job Redesign on the Assembly Line: Farewell to the Blue-Collar Blues?" by William Dowling, *Organizational Dynamics* 2:2 (Autumn, 1973), for a discussion of the economic conflict between specialization and participation, as well as an extensive account of several major job redesign efforts.

performance replicable without extensive management attention, management attention will necessarily focus on the routine. By the time of Du Pont and General Motors, the specification of task had moved from codifying workers' routine activities to codifying managers' routine activities.

It is through administrative systems that planning and policy are made possible, because the systems capture knowledge *about* the task, and, at the General Motors and Du Pont Levels, *about* the logically more inclusive matter of coordinating tasks. The return on assets concepts of Donaldson Brown, the forecasting methods, the systematic relation of demand, production, inventories, and appropriations all represent a methodology for managing, a directed way of thinking that translates a level upwards in a hierarchy of logic and inclusiveness from the single-factory, single-firm management concepts of Taylor and Church. Moreover, any manager who has been exposed to these methods has been trained in an administrative mechanism that explicitly guides perceptions and interpretation. In this, as in Taylor's concrete specifications of a machinist's task, a shared frame of reference is created. The firm is no longer dependent upon the rediscovery of these relations, every time, by each new manager. Instead, the knowledge of Donaldson Brown, Pierre du Pont, John Raskob, or Alfred P. Sloan, Jr., is codified and preserved. It is thereby made accessible to others, for both replication and further development. These administrative systems create a shared pattern of thought, with focus explicitly shifted to the *pattern*, rather than the specific content. They thus condition the analyses and decision premises of the actors. Specified kinds of thinking are identified. By creating a shared frame of reference, with explicitly directed perceptions—"The relation of finished goods inventory to customer demand should not exceed thus-and-such a ratio when scheduling production," for instance—such systems generalize knowledge far beyond its original discoverer or discovery situation. It should be emphasized here that the *kind* of knowledge generalized is qualitatively, logically different from the kind of knowledge codified in Taylor's machine-oiling instructions. The focus is on paths or patterns of thought and kinds of thinking, rather than on specific actions.

These systems, in generalizing the insights they codify, also make them accessible to change and refinement. It is no longer necessary for the procedures of a firm to be the work of a single mind. The systems, as Sloan's[4] comments make clear, measure results, leaving the details of task performance to others. Because management need pay attention only to these monitors, patterns among them and over time assume more importance. True management by exception, and true policy direction are now possible, solely because management is no longer wholly immersed in the details of the task itself. Having been guided into replicating the patterns of thought for connecting, say, production and inventory, it is now possible to add the refinements of forecasting demand, and of revising the forecasts or adjusting them in the light of general economic conditions and actual demand. Thus the original relationship, once comprehended, can be changed and shaped, transcended and surpassed. The development of flexible, rather than rote, responses to changing situations grew out of the new attention to the coordinative task made possible only because abstraction focused attention on anomalies in patterns. The systemic relationship among quantitative measures of performance and environmental indicators—substantially abstracted, be it noted, from details of task performance—is what permits control at this level.

Taylor was concerned primarily with individual tasks, or with a single work flow; Church, with the ongoing business of the firm as a whole, and with the relationships of individuals' tasks within that framework, with the coordination of the factory. Du Pont and General Motors are still more general, abstract, and logically inclusive, in that their methods of management relate diverse products typically produced by many factories. For Du Pont, applying accounting methods meant adapting the practices of the steel and traction industries to explosives manufacture, and later to chemicals. For General Motors, the task was adequately systematizing related but distinct products. More importantly, for both firms the task was generalizing patterns of thought that would permit decentralization. In both cases, the clear distinction between details of task performance and the coordination of those details, on the one hand, and the overarching coordinative task of relating *many* tasks (products, divisions, factories) was institutionalized not just in organization structure, but in the administrative systems that controlled information flow and guided critical decision making and analysis. The administrative systems capture the knowledge of how to think about this diversity, how to relate information about it (clearly an abstraction from the things themselves), how to coordinate and manage effectively. The shared frame of reference that is created is more inclusive, and therefore logically superior, to single-firm, single-factory frames of reference. By focusing attention on the abstractions, the systems encourage both replication of established patterns of thought—as relating inventory and production, for instance—and their refinement, keying in economic conditions or actual demand.

SYSTEMATIC INNOVATION AT TEXAS INSTRUMENTS

The chief accomplishment at Du Pont and General Motors was in systematizing the ongoing business of the large, complex, multidivisional firm. At Texas Instruments, the main task was (and is) of an altogether different nature. The highly changeful environment of modern electronics requires a new set of administrative systems designed to decentralize not only the performance of a routine task in a somewhat turbulent environment, but the decentralization of innovation itself, and with it the fundamental data-gathering of the policy process.

Texas Instruments provides a capsule history of the development of management theory, repeated in brief compass. The PCC System institutionalized and insisted upon a fundamental balance in the ongoing business. This might be called the basic task of the firm, systematized in ways that Church would find familiar. Coordinated management of the task required adequate controls, proper attention to the essential elements of product and customer, and to the fit between them. With the number of different products and markets, this brought TI to the level of General Motors and Du Pont in the evolution of its management systems.

The OST System is qualitatively different, and constitutes a further distinct logical shift. It is concerned with a higher logical level. Rather than coordinating multiple routine tasks, the OST is focused on generating new tasks which may eventually themselves become routine. Equally as important, it is concerned with generalizing a shared frame of reference, a means of acquiring new knowledge. As a system, the OST generalizes a procedure for acquiring the requisite new knowledge, creating a shared pattern of thought *regarding innovation* in much the same way that Du Pont or General Motors created shared frames of reference about ongoing business. The OST specifies how to proceed, monitor, and evaluate. In so doing, the OST makes it possible for Texas Instruments to acquire not only new products, but new paradigms or identities. Thus TI is not just a geophysical exploration company, but also a military instruments supplier; not just a geophysics and military instruments company, but also an electronics firm, and so on. Recent forays into consumer goods (calculators and watches) are indicative of a major capacity for change.

HIERARCHIES OF LEARNING

In *Steps to an Ecology of Mind,*[5] Gregory Bateson notes that learning, as a communication process, must be subject to the laws of cybernetics. He proceeds to make use of Russell's Theory of Logical Types in a behavioral science context. Thus the concepts of hierarchy, distinctions between logical classes or types, and their importance in guiding analysis suggest new ways of looking at learning phenomena. In particular, accurate class distinctions are essential for a meaningful discussion of learning. Bateson suggests that there are different types of learning, which may be arranged in a developmental hierarchy of progressively more inclusive frames of reference with systematic relationships between levels. Such a hierarchy highlights important distinctions among the administrative systems described above, retaining awareness of their similarities as shared frames of reference accessible to others. Such a hierarchy illuminates these administrative systems as varieties of codified learning.

Taking Bateson a step closer to organizations, Fenwick[6] defines a hierarchy of learning activities in an organization without, however, defining what "knowledge" or "learning" might be in an extra-individual context. Recasting these concepts in the light of the kinds of distinctions necessary to define organizational learning, we can take into account accessibility to others, preservation of knowledge, and a shared frame of reference. Thus we can:

1. Record the specifics of basic tasks;
2. Record the specifics of new tasks, and routinize them when they recur;
3. Generate approaches to analyzing and recording new tasks;
4. Extract the general principles of tasks, going beyond simple replication to efficiency, and possibly to generalized application of the new principles and efficiencies;
5. Develop programs for approaching new task areas, different from what has been routinized;
6. Evolve training programs to teach new approaches;
7. Shape or change the organization's mission or paradigm; and
8. Develop approaches for repeated or ongoing paradigm change.

What is the utility of defining so exhaustive a hierarchy? The distinctions facilitate a more precise discussion of *organizational* learning (as opposed to individual learning), and of organizational *learning* (as opposed to "mere adaptation"). Each level distinguishes a more far-reaching and thorough-going kind of change, with wider impact and longer-range consequences. Finally, this is a developmental sequence. Later levels rest upon the conceptual foundation of earlier levels, as the historical context provided by early chapters emphasizes.Until the managerial technology of Taylor and Church had been developed, the coordination sought by Du Pont and General Motors was impossible.

As Bateson points out, the Theory of Logical Types implies that in such a hierarchy each level constitutes a "meta-communication," that is, a communication "about" the next lower level and inclusive of all elements in it. This is particularly important in the organizational context, where the epistemology of moving from "subjective knowledge" to "objective knowledge"–the hinge between individual and organizational knowledge— turns upon just such a communication phenomenon. A shared frame of reference, relating lower-level elements and guiding their interpretation in order that similar stimuli result in similar results, is dependent in the organizational setting, upon some objective or shared knowledge. That is, it is dependent upon true communication, the sharing of a common frame of reference. This obviously goes beyond simple exchange of noise to shared understanding. The meta-communication, in other words, provides a common frame of reference within which a common understanding can be expected. This may, particularly in the complex organization, be compliated by diversity of interest or specialty, or by organization size or geographic dispersion, for instance. Organizational learning, despite these complications, must be a communication phenomenon. Only through communication does individual insight become accessible to others, and thereby transcend its discoverer, making possible synergy.

A hierarchy of types such as the one suggested provides a means of focusing attention on distinctions between levels, or, in the case of organizations, between systems. What matters is not that there are eight levels here, rather than the three individual-learning levels Bateson defines. What is important is the developmental nature of the sequence, and the assistance that these distinctions provide, helping to distinguish definitively between rote response in an organizational setting (even a complex rote response) and something more sophisticated. More important still, in delineating the distinction, the hierarchy suggests implicitly the criteria by which "learning" in organizations might be judged, the vocabulary with which such phenomena might be discussed, and the likely direction for systems evolution. On this basis, the already-established data base (Taylor, Church, Du Pont and General Motors, and Texas Instruments) shall be used to make the concept of organizational learning more clear.

THE HIERARCHY APPLIED

The lower reaches of the hierarchy set out here concern the areas of Taylor's work. While learning to perform any task is learning to perform a "new" task for the first time, the distinction gains importance in an organizational setting. Thus a basic task may be defined as one for which a program already exists. This is the kind of "knowledge" or "learning" that Cyert and March are willing to countenance in organizations. Taylor's contributions include both specification of particular knowledge (how to oil a machine) and ways to learn new tasks (ways for the organization to record and thereby retain new knowledge, fitting it into a system). The ideas of time and motion study, of noting elemental movements and aggregating them, of adequate description constitute a frame of reference, accessible to others, which specifies how to acquire and preserve new knowledge and expedite its transmission to others.

It is important to underline again the difference between individual and organizational learning. Clearly an individual can approach a task in a variety of ways. What Taylor has outlined is a way to record and transmit *organized* individual perceptions, making them both accessible to others and independent of the original observer. It is via the specified, shared frame of reference Taylor designates that these perceptions are removed from the subjective to the objective world. Knowledge so recorded and codified is no longer the preserve of the individual. And anyone following Taylor's procedures has gone through a series of guided observations whose recorded output is just such an "objective" record, comprehensible to others trained in the method. Hence the organization is no longer dependent wholly on serendipity or individual talent to create an approach to acquiring new knowledge; one has been specified. These rules provided a limited example of rules for learning. Taylor's metal-cutting experiments and Church's "organic functions" as well are logically superior, because they are more inclusive than the simple recording of observations. The overarching framework is a set of guides for interpretation and for relating many specific tasks. Their focus is extracting general principles and attaining efficiencies. General Motors and Du Pont are to be considered here too, as specifying general principles (abstractions) and noting efficient relationships among elements. Only through abstraction is more general coordination possible. Only through a shared frame of reference, generalized beyond the original discoverer, is such coordination feasible; and with it, something that can meaningfully be described as "organizational" learning.

The upper reaches of this hierarchy, beyond level three, concern just the types of "learning rules" that Cyert and March exclude from their consideration. Bateson's much less detailed hierarchy was intended for discussions of individual learning; but the same distinctions—with some adaptation to take into account the need for communication and extra-individual accessibility—are useful for a discussion of organizational learning. By considering the hierarchy in its logical sense, the problem of "structure" versus "process" becomes clearer, for example. For any level, the given level is "process," subject to change according to the *fixed* rules specified by levels above. The levels above are, therefore, "structure," and are the "learning rules" that Cyert and March exclude. The advantage of such a hierarchy is that it permits and encourages a richer view of the learning phenomena, and thus provides a more powerful model for considering them. The levels provide ranges of inclusiveness within which to assess the impact or pervasiveness of change. We can choose temporarily to see a certain level as structure, without wholly ignoring the possibility of change there, or in higher levels still, over a longer time frame. Similarly, higher levels correspond to corporate goals: shared frames of reference of far-reaching consequence, changeable only with major effort and over extensive time-horizons. Indeed, such flexibility would seem critical in dealing with learning, which must be a *change* phenomenon, longitudinal in its development. Thus, while the "learning rules" may change only slowly over time, they are, nonetheless, only *relatively* fixed. The matter of organization or patterning or arrangement is critical here in specifying rules and their application. The higher levels of the hierarchy are changeable, given the proper focus and time span. They are not excluded nor seen as wholly fixed. It is this distinction that allows a meaningful discussion of morphogenesis, for "change of shape" or restructuring must also be a long-term developmental phenomenon. Similarly too, in the largest sense, change of mission or paradigm is change of "shape," and can be explicitly included here. Such changes as these require an even longer time horizon and an even more inclusive frame of reference. Buckley's question[7] recurs: "The basic problem is the same: how do interacting personalities and groups define, assess, interpret, *verstehen*, and act on the situation?" In light of the foregoing discussion, the question can now be answered, in part at least, by means of the shared frames of reference created by administrative systems and the 'learning rules' they impound. It matters little that the initial insight was an individual's; the codification and communication of that insight, and its translation into a shared frame of reference transcend this origin by communicating the knowledge and preserving it.

Taylor and Church, in providing methods for systematizing or routinizing ongoing business, illustrate level two: routinizing already-learned procedures so that success in what was once a "new" task can be replicated. Replicability, predictability, and thus increased control over the myriad details of concrete task performance were central to one aspect of the work of the systematic management thinkers. Another aspect, that of efficiency and general principles (clearly visible in the writings of both Taylor and Church) is of a higher logical level. The distinction is important, because it determines the criteria on which the procedure is to be judged. Simple replication might well be fortuitous; it certainly smacks of the Black Box with wired-in connections. It is not evidence of "learning" in any meaningful sense. Generating approaches to new tasks is different.* A format for approaching new tasks by making possible the continued acquisition of new knowledge repeats a process, rather than its content. It generalizes principles or relationships among elements, guiding thinking. This goes well beyond replication of content. Extracting general principles and generalizing efficiency methods would seem clear evidence of learning,

---

*While "the task" might be redefined anew at each level—as "analyzing the specifics of a new transformation element and recording them" at level two, for instance—such a redefinition is far less useful than maintaining the distinction between "the task" as the work peformed at the primary level by a given worker, and various coordinative activities that take place elsewhere, upwards in the managerial hierarchy. By reserving "task" to the activities of Thompson's (1967) "technological core," we can conform more closely to ordinary usage. And it is far easier to signal a shift in focus to managerial activities, as distinct from whatever transformations are carried out to produce the firm's output of goods or services. Other usages are possible; this usage appears to me to be the most useful for my purposes.

rather than mere iteration. Built into a system in Taylor's work-simplification methods, or Church's management systems, they would be evidence
of organizational learning, because they would be accessible far beyond the
discoverer. Similarly, the Du Pont and General Motors management information systems and the controls upon which they rest generalize and
communicate principles and relationships which are applied to the business
of the corporation as a whole (including to new products) to gain efficiencies. Thus, for instance, reducing the cash tied up in divisional bank
accounts by arranging for the speedy transfer of funds was a general
application of the principle of increasing return by increasing turnover of
inventories—including "inventories" of cash.

INSTITUTIONALIZING INNOVATION

Of far greater interest from the viewpoint of innovation are levels
higher still: developing programs for approaching new task areas, teaching
the approaches, changing the paradigm of the organization, and developing
approaches for repeated change. From one perspective, these are iterations of the "new approaches" methods but applied to innovation, rather
than to the routines of the task. From another viewpoint they are the stuff
of policy decisions, concerning, as they do, questions of long-range proactiveness, institutional identity and change. In an era of increasing rates of
technological and social change, they are, therefore, critically important
concepts. Any theory that facilitates our thinking about them, describing
them and, perhaps, making them occur more readily would be worthwhile.

The history of Texas Instruments centers on these higher levels of the
hierarchy of learning, even as General Motors and Du Pont centered
primarily on levels three and four. The wartime experiences of the predecessor firm, GSI, involved going into a new task area. GSI redirected the
specific knowledge of geophysics upon which Magnetic Airborne Detectors were based, but also developed programs for selling to the military,
and for manufacturing instruments for the use of others outside the firm.
The firm was small, however, and much of this could be carried on by one
man, or a few. After the war, the decision to shift into instruments manufacture as a second line of business, rather than merely a survival strategy,
was a paradigm shift. Just as expanding into new areas is an activity at a
higher, more inclusive logical level than learning to do a new, but related
task, so, too, changing the firm's mission, identity, or paradigm is more
inclusive than adding a new, but related product. The model of the firm
("GSI is a geophysical service firm") changed to "We manufacture instruments which we sell—geophysical and military; *and* we are a geophysical
service firm." This shaping or changing of paradigm (level seven in the
hierarchy) was primarily the work of Erik Jonnson and Patrick Haggerty,
as individuals. While learning took place, and was eventually impounded in

the shift of field, the expansion of manufacturing, and the acquisition of new personnel to implement the shift, it might be argued that what occurred was still essentially individual learning. But by this time the firm had about 100 employees in the manufacturing division alone, and many oldtimers remained. Clearly the new knowledge was not the preserve of either Haggerty or Jonsson alone.

The establishment of a manufacturing division and the pursuit of military business constitute a clear instance of institutionalizing individual insights. A shared frame of reference, guiding perceptions, providing expectations, and assisting interpretations, had come to exist. New ways of approaching the tasks of electronics instrumentation and components manufacture, aimed at volume production and outside customers, rather than at producing enough for the service arm of the company, were developed and codified, in keeping with the new dual paradigm. Structural recognition in and of itself helped create the shared frame of reference.

The product-line decentralization of the company, in 1954, represents a further explicit recognition of the TI commitment to diversified manufacture in electronics. At about the same time, the decision to go into semiconductors was made. This decision, like the decision to pursue military contracts, or to sell geophysical instruments to outside customers, was deliberately, explicitly made. Haggerty emphasized the choice involved:*

> I remember when I first used to call on Phillips overseas—among many of the oldtimers we had friends—the thing that I suppose amazed them most, and amused them most, was that we went into semiconductors *deliberately*. Almost everyone else that went into semiconductors either were already in vacuum tubes and it was a logical outgrowth; or it was people who had been trained technically in the field. What amazed and amused them was, "You mean you really just *thought* about what you ought to be doing, and picked semiconductors, even though you hadn't done any work in the field? And didn't have any people who were trained?" Yes, that's exactly what we did.

Nor was this procedure extraordinary, for Texas Instruments. Indeed, Haggerty thought it was typical of the firm's practice.

> But you see, that was characteristic of us, really. In the sense of thinking out what you really were there for, what you thought you wanted to be in the future, and what it would take to get there.

---

*Personal interview, 1976. All citations of Haggerty, unless otherwise identified, refer to this series.

Explicit attention to the long-term direction of the firm—the firm's paradigm, in the vocabulary of this study—requires a frame of reference inclusive enough to meaningfully contemplate alternatives. Such a focus has been characteristic of the top levels of the firm, institutionalized by prolonged attention and effort on the part of Haggerty, among others.

> I think that the other thing that was characteristic before OST was recognized formally was this business of planning the future. We started with our first formal planning conference in 1952. We had had informal ones in my office for a few years before that. It had *always* been more than budgeting. Initially, it was only a year or two at a time; a year in detail, and then a couple of years past it in not very much detail. And it's true that it always ended up with the numbers and the budgets. But we were really much more concerned with products, services, customers, where were we going, growth rates, where was the third leg coming from, and all the rest of that. And we had the first formal planning conference in 1952.

It may well be true that few firms do any strategic planning (that matters), as Cyert and March suggest; it is clearly not the case that *no* firms do such planning. In this context, TI's proactive stance is not to be underestimated. The nature of the technological effort in developing the silicon transistor and the choice of a pocket radio as a means of creating a market to force costs, prices, and demand were clearly purposeful strategies, directed toward a recognized end. Just as clearly, the luxury of attention to such high levels of abstraction rests upon a thoroughly institutionalized means of decentralizing and delegating the ongoing business of the firm. As well, the firm must be envisioned within a paradigm that includes alternative futures. If the frame of reference is not sufficiently abstracted and generalized from the obvious "now," no concerted effort is possible toward creating a future, rather than merely experiencing what comes, willy-nilly.

Haggerty's impetus is visible throughout. But the direction of the company and its successes are by no means his achievement alone, nor his only achievement. A greater success is to be seen in the creation of an administrative system—the OST—which decentralizes the modes of thinking and the patterns of action by which he directed the firm. This system, by impounding and institutionalizing Haggerty's insights, expanded the approach beyond the man himself, permitting a new level of synergy. Far more "new task" activity and far more projects, as well as more alternative futures, became possible with this generalized system than Haggerty himself could possibly have provided. Haggerty repeatedly described the OST as a formal means of accomplishing what had been handled informally when the firm was small. In the old days, without a system, innovation did happen. It was personally directed.

It was working, but that's because, fundamentally, I could *do* it; we were small enough. I don't mean to imply that I was the only one doing it, but there were only 8 or 10 other people who were in positions of responsibility, and I could see every single one of them, every single day. You didn't have to have OST meetings and all the rest of it. You could damn well *see* that you paid attention to those 8 or 10 programs. As you get bigger, that's not feasible.

What Haggerty is describing is the close personal supervision that lets one manager coordinate, personally drawing the diverse and divergent activities together and monitoring the fit and balance among them. He could personally insure that projects remained on track, were coordinated, that ideas from one area were meshed with ideas from another, and that close coupling did indeed take place. As the firm grew larger and more complex, in direct parallel to the situation of the metal working industry of the 1890s (though here concerned with new projects), Haggerty alone could no longer provide all of the necessary coordination and monitoring. To continue to grow, TI needed many more than the eight or ten projects he could personally supervise. The company needed a system to substitute for Haggerty's personal surveillance.[8]

The level of abstraction is imperative here. It distinguishes between *doing* the new business management, and *directing* it. Level three, generating approaches to new tasks, is very different from level two, learning to perform new tasks. The distinct shift required by increasing complexity was of a higher order of logic still, for the new approaches Haggerty had successfully applied now had to be generalized. Their principles had to be extracted, and means found to teach them to others, making them accessible beyond the coterie that a single manager could personally coordinate. Only when the insights were made accessible to others, applied *and refined by them*, were they truly *organizational* learning, rather than simply Haggerty's own. Thus the OST as an administrative system is a mechanism for institutionalizing learning rules.

Codifying the system guided others explicitly and objectively in the pattern of thought Haggerty himself had led people through informally. The codification is essential, in rendering the knowledge independent of its inventor, in this case, Haggerty. It provides an administrative, organizational means for accomplishing the same coupling formerly attained by proximity, by close personal supervision, or by good luck; as Haggerty noted:

The OST system does that superbly. It clearly, better than anything else I have seen, provides this coupling in a much bigger and more complex organization than a few of us could provide personally when you could walk from one laboratory to another, and work 70 or 80 hours a week, and you knew everybody, and knew as fast as they thought of something what they were thinking of, and what the problems were. All this is, is a mechanism which does that same thing, and *forces* you to do it on a regular basis. It is tightening the coupling, improving the odds that you will recognize this hook, and this one . . . as having some relevance, or some interference, and doing something about it.

CHANGING ADMINISTRATIVE LEARNING

Codification is essential for yet another reason. If the new knowledge is to be truly institutionalized, truly organizational rather than individual, then others besides the inventor must use it, and change it to suit new organizational realities. This process most clearly took place repeatedly with the OST early on, as the approach was shaped to connect OST practices to other management systems in place; and later, as different executives rose to general management positions in new circumstances.

One such change was the addition of the IDEA System or the "wild hare" program. This change was a direct response to continued growth, and to the formalism of major innovative projects. The IDEA System supports less well formulated and more risky ventures, particularly those in formative stages. As the company grew, TI faced constraints on the downside as to the programs it could back. To keep the relative impact of OST programs high, so that they would be truly strategic, the absolute size of projects had to increase. Haggerty commented on the phenomenon.

It's an old saw in the oil business: a big oil company has to find big oil fields; a little company can find little oil fields. That's one of the good things about the OST System—we can't afford too many small projects. That's a thing that drives the boys crazy, the young ones, because very frequently, their ideas are *good* ideas. But when you examine them, it looks as if the impact couldn't be enough on the company. So you never pursue them. You pursue some other thing, which might be more mundane . . . but which, if it succeeds, is of large enough impact to be significant. Now if that's *all* you do, you're wrong, too. So you have to have enough programs which can be started with only six or ten people. Nearly always the essence of something can be solved by them. Effectively, if you've *got* to work with too many people, you've again decreased the odds, considerably.

In talking about the OST, you're talking about directed work. . . . The other thing you'd better have is a certain amount of relatively free work going on. And you control it by how much money you put into it. But because it is wasteful—and it *is* wasteful—the better managers you develop over the years, the more likely they are to keep looking at that and not being very happy with it, wanting to focus it tightly.

One source of "free-wheeling" ideas is centrally located, corporate funded research of a "frankly exploratory" nature. But such programs must be limited. The IDEA System is intended to supplement this with a means of funding boot-strap, bench-level innovative thinking.

The IDEA System is clearly a variant of the original OST methodology, a systematic approach to innovation. It is also clearly a refinement or correction—a means of beating the constraints imposed by the "big oil company, big oil fields" syndrome that would seem inevitable. The IDEA System works with less formality, less control, less information. Yet, like the OST, it is explicitly goal-directed and commercially aimed. The name, IDEA, is an acronym for *Identify, Develop, Expose* and *Action*. The system is supposed to *identify* ideas which might have commercial potential; supply funding for short-term efforts to *develop* enough information to justify more formal, more serious and longer-term exploration; *expose* the developed idea to top levels (the Corporate Development Committee); and initiate *action* by feeding the newly developed idea into the OST System for further development and commercialization. The IDEA System strongly resembles the OST of very early days in its informality and the access it provides to top levels.

As with OST and P&AE projects, IDEA projects may be technically or nontechnically oriented. However, to qualify for funding they must be "step advances" or significant changes, not just evolutionary developments, either of products, processes or business methods. The anticipated scope of an IDEA project is four to six months, with funding provided for purchasing needed services and materials for proving feasibility. However, the originator of the project cannot charge his own time: "The purpose of the IDEA funds is to provide funding to demonstrate the feasibility of an IDEA; it is not to divert the efforts of the IDEA originator from his present tasks."[9]

Like the OST and P&AE systems, approval requires a written statement of the approach, impact or application if successful, an estimate of expenses and time required, and a goal statement of what the output would be (demonstration model, paper analysis, etc.). Review is limited to ascertaining whether the end result falls within the business interests of TI, and whether there is not a similar project underway elsewhere in the firm. Other than that, the idea originator need merely convince an IDEA person, who need not be in the originator's division. An originator may approach more than one IDEA person, but needs convince only one to set the system in motion.

To an even greater extent than the OST, the IDEA System is an alternate access route to funding, to the attention of the top levels of the corporation and its policy makers. It provides for more ready access into the planning procedure than a low-level technician, say, might otherwise have. As a true alternate, it supplements more formalized systems, rather than replacing them.

Changes like the addition of the IDEA System to fill in for the informal encouragement available in earlier days are part and parcel of the effort to institutionalize or build in the OST. Haggerty referred to the need for this kind of effort and attention to connections.

○   I think this is one of the principles: if you think something is important, you had better find *some* way of building into the organization *the necessity* to solve those problems. If you examine most of our systems, the reason the OST works here and won't necessarily work at very many places is because, after trying like hell, and keeping it up for a very long time, we got it built into the system, so it's the only way you can get anything done around here. It's the ONLY WAY! Unless you do it that way, you're not going to get your money, you're not going to get it done.

▫   What Haggerty and others at TI refer to as "getting it built into the system" is much akin to what Murray calls "administrative knowledge,"[10] in its formal aspects. Explicitly creating performance expectations, specifically delineating acceptable procedure, linking performance in the new networks with evaluation and advancement, and providing formal rewards for users of the new network serve to integrate the behavioral requirements with the formal means for organizational control. The notion is similar to some of Kerr's ideas as well:[11] what you take into account (and therefore, what you reward) is what you get, in administrative systems terms. Haggerty expounded further:

In a much simpler environment, I found out that systems were somewhat extraneous, and things you did if managers were intelligent enough to know that the systems aided them, but that they didn't have to do in order to achieve their ends, were quite likely not to be very successful systems. I learned that on production control systems, which are very much simpler. So right from the beginning, we sought, in designing systems, to do it in such a way that if they didn't do it *that* way, they didn't get what *they wanted*. A thing as simple as a production control system, when you first install it, is a headache. Because it's different from what you're doing, it doesn't work very well at the beginning. They have more trouble than they had before, so they tend to do both things at once. They know that; they only do *this* 'cause they're *told* to. And it doesn't succeed that way. So what you really had to figure out, was a closed loop of some kind, where unless they did it *all*, they didn't get what they wanted. You had to see that the pieces of paper were an absolute link. And make it simple enough so that it wasn't too bad—but that they had to take all the steps. If they took those steps, then they got what they wanted. If they didn't take the steps, they didn't get what they wanted—unless they went to a hell of a lot of effort circumventing everything.

> Now, it's much harder to do with something like an OST System. It requires absolute involvement and collaboration from the top down. In fact, that's the principle of the system, that it is done by those people who are responsible for the success of the organization—not by a bunch of staff people. We *insist* on the top people themselves being involved in it. This is the way it's worked from the beginning. It is a way of organizing *their* time with respect to the future. And forcing it, forcing it, forcing it, forcing it. It took a long time. It took a LONG time!

Murray's data, suggesting seven to ten years from the idea to full implementation, are mirrored in TI's experience, according to Haggerty.

> It took a long time, and a lot of false starts. We introduced it in 1962, but boy, it was 1969 before it was really working. Except in some places . . . it worked right away in some places; in others, it took a long time, for just that reason. It was that long before all of the people who counted were really getting what they wanted via that route.
>
> I think that's an essential to the evolution of any system, anywhere. It has to be the way the place is run. It has to be the way the place HAS to be run, if they're going to get their odds. Now, that means if you're wrong about the system, you know, you've really hung a bad one on the organization. If you're right about it, then it'll work, and you'll get on from there.

The IDEA System, various administrative linkages and changes, and the like are less fundamental singly than in concert. The most profound change, that represented by the P&AE System, is most clearly the result of organizational learning or institutionalization of the OST. Codification had made the OST accessible for refinement, and refined it was. An important shift took place, making the OST "organizational" in its genesis, as well as in its application. As he described it, Haggerty's original conception of the OST was decidedly limited in scope.

> As I envisioned the OST in the first place, it was going to be used to do all of the new things, the new programs, and consequently we might use OST in a third to a half of our business. Not in the sense that we'd use it in one place and not in another, but that as a thing became routine, it wouldn't be handled under OST. OST would be the way that you did what amounted to your programmatic things, until they became part of the business, and then you got them out of the OST. Fundamentally, I suppose, that's the way the silicon transistor had been done, that's the way the pocket radio had been done, that's how we handled our approach with digital programming, geophysics, and so forth.

Other managers—Haggerty's successors—saw the system more inclusively, more globally, he noted:

> The enormous thing that both Bucy and Shepherd saw . . . was that that [programmatic] approach wouldn't work, and for the obvious reason that I started with. The only way something that complicated works . . . is to build it in.

Because the task of innovation has to be decentralized, the approach or methodology has to be of a piece with other aspects of the management system. Consistency, and systemic interrelation or linkage are critical. The approach couldn't be partial:

> It's not that Bucy and Shepherd set out to make it a part of the culture. It's that in contemplating what was wrong and what they did that I recognized that difference in what Bucy was saying . . . as long as we only did it in some places, about some things—"We don't keep our books that way, except on these programs"—it was too easy for them to run their businesses the other way and then only operate this way when I am standing on top of them, asking "What are you doing about this program?"

The successive refinements in the OST were the contributions of Bucy and Shepherd, who insisted that the system be more broadly applied:

> What they said was, "Although it's much harder, it's the only way." And they recognized that I started it the other way. The OST is *difficult*. There *is* paperwork; there *is* discipline; you *do* have to have meetings, you *do* have to force people to get together. Because the whole idea is this business of sessions and meetings, and this business of reducing the odds because you make the hooks visible, and all that. So as I saw it initially, it was going to be on the big things, the things that were going to change the business, the things that you were trying to get done for next year, and three years from now, and ten years from now. That was the reason that it took from 1962 to 1969. The reason it finally succeeded was because they saw very clearly that it had to happen in the whole business.

Building it into the culture" is the way Haggerty and others spoke of institutionalizing the OST. With the concepts of hierarchy and inclusiveness in mind, the systemic nature of the required relationships between the OST and the rest of the company becomes apparent. The changes required are far-reaching and quite inclusive, having to do with generalizing a fundamental approach to knowledge. This is why "It took a long time, and a lot of false starts."

What it means to have such a system "built into the culture" relates to the distinction between individual and organizational learning. Murray documents the experience of banks in developing a new line of business, loans to minority groups.[12] He concludes that there is a critical difference between "technical knowledge" (the sheer knowledge of how to accomplish a specific task) and "administrative knowledge," which is formally institutionalized and integrated into the organization. One aspect of the difference concerns generalizing the insight or practice by codifying it in order that it may be generalized beyond the original discoverers. A second, equally important, aspect concerns motivating the use of this new knowledge—making it a part of the shared frame of reference that is drawn upon by other organization members. Not only must the knowledge be accessible to others; it must also be congruent with other explicit expectations, practices, and procedures of the firm. In order to pass beyond the individual's "Aha!," or the joint discovery of a small band of specialist explorers, knowledge must be operationalized in practice. That is, it must be formalized into an administrative system that is as legitimate and as important as other procedural guides that affect the organization members' shared frame of reference. It was this that Haggerty was emphasizing in underlining the need to insure that "all the people who counted were really getting what they wanted" through the new system. The thoroughgoing nature of such a change is obvious: "If you're wrong about the system, you know, you've really hung a bad one on the organization." To make a system work, to make it "the way the place HAS to be run," it must be totally integrated. This way must be "the ONLY way" to get things done. It becomes clear that "building the system into the culture," making it *necessary* to people, involves making it consistent with other procedures, expectations, ways of thinking, modes of operation, and means of evaluating performance. It is consistency with a multitude of other subsystems, not just internal consistency, that matters.

With the OST, a system for directing approaches to new business, the integration process was far more complex than that required for routine business systems. First, of course, there was "Gresham's Law"—the imperative demands of ongoing business had a tendency to drive out the nonroutine. In addition, because the procedures and results could not be specified in advance, or even specified in general, monitoring was more difficult. Instead, the parameters, measures, and criteria must vary with the task at hand, and the nature of the tasks themselves is unknown. Thus definition of measurement criteria must be delegated, along with the actual attainment of results. The OST does this, by insisting that those who have operational responsibility for the company run the OST as well. Those who do, plan; those who plan, do.

A THEORETICAL PERSPECTIVE AND SOME SPECULATIONS

This study has suggested that "organizational learning" must be defined more rigorously than by loose analogy with individual cognitive processes if it is to be useful or meaningful. Weber's cautions against reifying the organization, no less than Silverman's reminder that only individuals ever think or act, compel a more closely reasoned usage of the term, if it is to be used at all.

To define "organizational learning" more closely, a distinction must be drawn between individual and organizational learning, and between learning and "mere adaptation," the simple repetition of a predefined sequence of actions. Administrative systems—the formal codification of what may, initially, have been individual insights—offer a reasonable distinction between organizational and individual learning. What is codified is accessible; it is no longer the preserve of the original discoverer. In this context, however, some indication is required that what has been codified has truly been institutionalized. It is not enough, for a rigorous criterion of "organizational learning," that simple replication of previously successful actions occur. In addition, the application of successful patterns to new or changed situations, and the adaptation or change of the patterns themselves, preferably by others than the initial discoverer(s), are proposed as tests. When an insight has been used in a new situation with continuing success, evidence exists that the insight (and not merely a simple repetition) has been institutionalized. When an insight has been shaped and changed, or generalized to a new class of problem, still stronger evidence suggests that the insight can meaningfully be said to belong to the organization, rather than to the individual who first discovered it.

Clearly *some* organizational learning may escape our notice within this framework. Much of what an organization "knows" is not codified or formalized; instead, it is part of the culture, part of what is "understood." Yet what is codified and formalized in administrative systems *does* transcend the individual, it *is* accessible to others, and *can* be shaped, changed, and generalized. Moreover, where the administrative system in question is consistent with other practice in the organization it operates to create and reinforce a shared frame of reference. This guides expectations and definitions of what is acceptable, of what is important, of what is to be done, or thought, or attended to. This makes sense of the synergy which is the prime reason for creating organizations in the first place, without losing sight of the fundamental truth that individuals make up organizations. In so doing, the explanation offers a resolution of the structure/process quandary: "learning rules" are structure, but they are only *relatively* fixed. Over a longer time-frame, they, too, can be considered as "process" and moveable. This insight permits the discussion to take into account the distinguishing characteristic of organizations which separates them definitively from either mechanisms or organisms—their morphogenetic ability to change their shape. In this context, "shape" includes identity, paradigm, or mission, in addition to the more obvious structural definition (of divisions, factories, departments, or other organizational arrangements).

How, then, do organizations "learn"? They learn by codifying individual insights, thus making them accessible to others for adoption, true adaptation, change, and generalized application. The hierarchy of learning proposed here, from learning basic or routine tasks through generating learning systems and approaches to morphogenesis or paradigm change, facilitates a distinction between simple repetition and the logically distinct pattern replication of higher levels. Organizations learn differently at different levels of the hierarchy. What is specifiable, capable of codification in detail, and well understood* can be recorded and thus organizationally "remembered." That is, it can be retained and made accessible in explicit instructions, beyond the individual—à la Taylor. At higher levels, what is specified is not content but procedure. At the highest levels, the form of the oganization itself (its paradigm or structure) itself becomes "process," as the focus of change.

The issue, at higher levels, is institutionalizing and thereby generalizing, not the specific actions of lower levels but patterns of thought—the shared frame of reference. As March and Simon suggest[13] (but do not discuss or develop), innovation can be institutionalized. But it seems clear that what has to be built into the organization is a common vision of the organization as subject to the change-activities of its members—as capable of fundamental shape-changing in response to purposeful effort. This view goes well beyond any simple stimulus-response analysis of organizational change.

Such a shared frame of reference seems to exist at Texas Instruments. The result has been the genesis of important expectations and anticipations regarding the organization's mission. For TI at least, the shape of the organization—whether defined as the number of PCCs, the administrative systems of management, the corporate committees, or the industries, or businesses, or markets—is conspicuously and explicitly subject to purposive revision or change. (Following Norman's distinction,[14] the nature of changes contemplated and undertaken includes "reorientation" as well as "revision.") "We went into semiconductors deliberately." Since this is built into a shared frame of reference which includes the technology for such change, "we can undertake entirely new lines of business as well as revisions and extensions of old lines." Not only does the organization

---

*These qualifiers must instantly bring to mind Charles Perrow's typologies of technology. The concept here is of technology as knowledge or "know-how," rather than just hardware. Thus there is a "technology" of management; its "hardware" would be systems for management or administrative programs, "soft-ware" more appropriately, not machines. Perrow, "A Framework for the Comparative Analysis of Organizations," *American Sociological Review*, Vol. 32 (1967), pp. 194–208.

change its shape; the structural change is consciously directed and examined, and a vocabulary generated for describing the process.

The resultant pattern of thinking is analogous to Taylor in that it is an administrative system impounding a specific insight. It is analogous to Church, in that its focus is coordination. It is like the General Motors and Du Pont systems in that it is managerial and abstract, permitting delegation of the critical process. Step by step, it includes and transcends each of these levels, however. Since it is focused on innovation, and, more especially, on sufficiently broad-spectrum innovation that morphogenesis is the issue, the analogies can be carried to a new level. What the system provides is a frame of reference for dealing with repeated paradigm change. In a sense, it creates a readiness for ongoing paradigm shifts. The "structure" is no longer seen as immutable or outside the logical limits of contemplation and purposive change.

The multilevel change activity contained in Texas Instruments' administrative systems bears strong resemblance to the model that Beer[15] proposes for the proactive firm. On one level, the present, internal "now" of ongoing business is managed. On a higher level—as appropriate to the logically superior, systemic nature of the task—the external "futures" of the firm are actively considered, contemplated, and managed. On a third level, still higher, the present and the future are coordinated in a transcendent meta-model of the firm (see Figure 6.1).

However, Texas Instruments has explicitly split out another function in the P&AE System. This system looks to the refinement of present management systems. It seeks efficiency and increased productivity from both human and capital resources. This adds a fourth level, between Beer's operations and development boards, focused on making the present system better. Thus one level controls the system for the standard task, the ongoing business of the firm. A governor-level, logically superior, attends to the adequacy of this system. At this level, the question might be stated as, "How shall we adapt and refine *this* system, to make it better?" or, "Are we doing things right?" A higher governor questions whether the standard task itself should not be changed, abandoned, expanded, or metamorphosed: "Are we doing the right things?" This is the paradigm level. And the final level, governor to the others and consequently superior to them, coordinates in the largest sense between the present and the future: "If we keep doing this, will it continue to be right?" (see Figure 6.2).

Like Parsons' concept of qualitatively different managerial functions at different levels in the organizational hierarchy,[16] this schema guides our attention to important differences in the focus and nature of the management task. By calling attention to distinct systems, the schema suggests the need for systemic discontinuities—the need to split out these tasks "structurally," explicitly recognizing hierarchies of inclusiveness and dif-

FIGURE 6.1

Beer's Three-Level Model

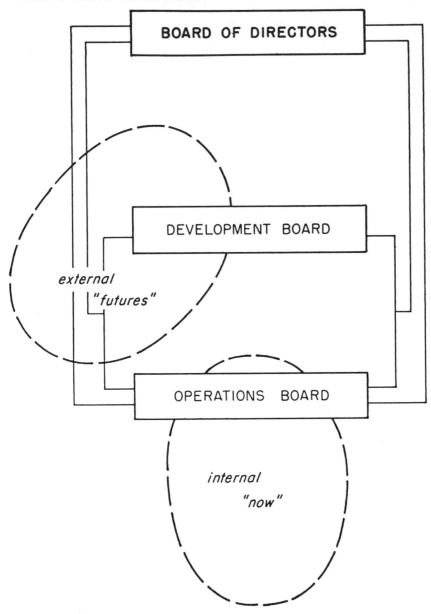

Source: Adapted by the author from S. Beer, *Platform for Change* (New York: Wiley, 1975).

FIGURE 6.2

Four-Level Model of Texas Instruments

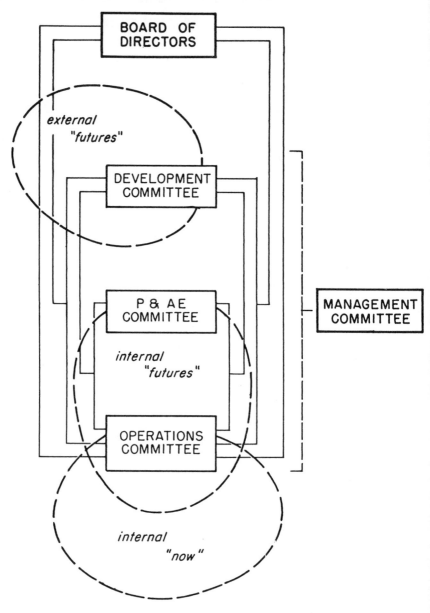

Source: Constructed by the author.

ferences of focus. Progressively longer time horizons, and distinctive perspectives are required.

The major question of whether the insights institutionalized at Texas Instruments can be generalized or not remains to be tested. It would seem clear that simple adoption of the *mechanisms* of OST planning into other organizations is unlikely to succeed. This is the case not merely because of "culture shock," but on the basis of systemic discontinuities, insuffiient logical place or authority in the hierarchy of systems, improperly narrow focus, too short time horizons, and the like. It is the logical charcter of the OST that must be adopted if such a transplant is to succeed. Further, it may well be that entirely different methods of significant forward planning exist in practice. Obviously, comparisons and the search for conceptual similarities between other such systems and the OST must await discovery and description. It may well be that similarities like the "cultural" congruence mentioned so often at Texas Instruments will turn up with regularity. Investigation of the nature of that congruence in a number of firms would seem fruitful, in that case. Both the experience of Texas Instruments and that of the banks investigated by Murray suggest that it would be most helpful to know just how cultural congruence is established. In other words, how can a system like the OST be "built into the culture"?

A final major issue centers on the question of whether significant planning can take place *except* in a system thoroughly integrated with the ongoing business of the firm. This question is surely of sufficient importance to warrant investigation. TI's experience seems to suggest that it cannot, and the absence of thoroughgoing integration may be one explanation for the dearth of successful significant planning noted by Cyert and March. This must have substantial implications for the staff planning departments and specialists in organizations, no less than for the way that the planning process is theoretically described, or taught.

Another way of summarizing might be to ask, "If there were such a thing as organizational learning, how would we know it existed?" I suggest that evidence of it would look very much like the administrative systems described in this study. To be *organizational*, rather than individual, learning, knowledge must be accessible to others beyond the discoverer, subject to both their application or use, and to their change and adaptation. Some formal means of transcending the initial discoverer would surely be evidence of such learning, even though learning and transmission of it to others may occur informally. Organizational learning, to be learning rather than "mere adaptation," must be generalized. It must go beyond simple replication to application, change, refinement. It must include "rules for learning" and their change and adaptation, rather than the rote iteration of past successful actions. It should, as proof of such change, be again applied to situations not met before, or met unsuccessfully, by these rules in the past. Finally, if learning is to include innovation, it must encompass a system for governing the future, as well as the present. In any case, organizational learning will be a communication phenomenon, a means of administering the interface between the individual and the organization.

Administrative systems to meet these specifications do indeed exist, at varying levels of complexity and inclusiveness. Organizations do plan significantly for the future. They seek to control their future environmental relations, as well as their present, and they shape themselves deliberately in order to do so. To speak meaningfully of organizational learning, we need not reify, we need not abandon the powerful insights of systems thinking, and we need not ignore the importance of the individual as actor. Administrative systems are the mechanisms for impounding and preserving knowledge. They create a shared frame of reference to make feasible the general application, refinement, and extension of such knowledge.

NOTES

1. James G. March and Herbert Simon. *Organizations* (New York: Wiley, 1959).

2. Richard Cyert and James G. March. *A Behavioral Theory of the Firm* (Englewood Cliffs, N.J.: Prentice-Hall, 1963).

3. March and Simon, *Organizations*, p. 185.

4. Alfred P. Sloan, Jr. *My Years with GM* (Garden City, N.Y.: Doubleday, 1972), pp. 162 ff.

5. Gregory Bateson. *Steps Toward an Ecology of Mind* (New York: Ballentine, 1972).

6. Noble James Fenwick, "Organizational Management of New Knowledge: A Case Study of a State Bureaucracy," Dissertation, MIT, 1975.

7. Walter Buckley. *Sociology and Modern Systems Theory* (Englewood Cliffs, N.J.: Prentice-Hall, 1967).

8. This is the same phenomenon described (albeit with somewhat different emphases) by William Rushing in "Organizational Rules and Surveillance: Propositions in Comparative Organizational Analysis," *Administrative Science Quarterly* 10:4 (March 1966), pp. 423–43.

9. Charles Phipps, Corporate Development, "The IDEA System," June, 1974. Copyright 1974 by Texas Instruments Incorporated.

10. Edwin A. Murray, "The Implementation of Social Policies in Commercial Banks," D.B.A. Dissertation, Graduate School of Business, Harvard University, 1974.

11. Steven Kerr. "On the Folly of Rewarding A, While Hoping for B," *Academy of Management Journal* 18 (Dec. 1975), 769–83.

12. Edwin A. Murray. "The Implementation of Social Policies in Commercial Banks" and "The Social Response Process in Commercial Banks: An Empirical Investigation," *The Academy of Management Review*, 1 (July 1976).

13. March and Simon, *Organizations*, p. 185.

14. Richard Norman. "Organizational Innovativeness: Product Variation and Reorientation," *Administrative Science Quarterly* (June 1971).

15. Stafford Beer. *Platform for Change* (New York: Wiley, 1975).

16. Talcott Parsons. *Structure and Process in Modern Societies* (Glencoe, Ill.: The Free Press of Glencoe, 1960). See also Joseph A. Litterer, *The Analysis of Organizations*, 2nd ed. (New York: Wiley, 1973), Ch. 22, for a discussion of similar distinctions in managerial focus.

BIBLIOGRAPHY

Andrews, Kenneth R. *The Concept of Corporate Strategy*. Homewood, Ill.: Dow Jones–Irwin, 1971.

Ashby, W. Ross. *Design for a Brain*. London: Chapman & Hall and Science Paperbacks, second edition, reprinted 1972.

————. *An Introduction to Cybernetics*. London: Chapman & Hall and Science Paperbacks, reprinted 1971.

Babbage, Charles. "On the Division of Labour," reprinted from *On The Economy of Machinery and Manufactures* (Philadelphia: Carey & Lea, 1832) in *Classics in Management*, ed. Harwood F. Merrill (American Management Association, n.p., 1970).

Barnard, Chester I. *The Functions of the Executive*. Cambridge: Harvard University Press, 1968. First published in 1938.

Baruch, Jordan. "The Management of Process Change: Lever on Productivity." Mimeographed. Graduate School of Business Administration, Harvard University, 1972.

Bateson, Gregory. *Steps Toward an Ecology of Mind*. New York: Ballentine, 1972.

Beer, Stafford. *Platform for Change*. New York: Wiley, 1975.

Buckley, Walter. *Sociology and Modern Systems Theory*. Englewood Cliffs, N.J.: Prentice-Hall, 1967.

Chandler, Alfred D., Jr., and Stephen Salsbury. *Pierre S. du Pont and the Making of the Modern Corporation*. New York: Harper and Row, 1977.

————. *Strategy and Structure*. Cambridge: The MIT Press, 1962.

————. *Giant Enterprise: Ford, General Motors and the Automobile Industry*. New York: Harcourt, Brace and World, 1964.

Church, Alexander Hamilton. "The Meaning of Commercial Organization," *Engineering Magazine* 20 (1900), 392–93. Cited in Joseph A. Litterer, "Alexander Hamilton Church and the Development of Modern Management," *Business History Review*, 35 (Summer 1961), p. 213.

————. *The Science and Practice of Management*. New York: The Engineering Magazine Co., 1914.

————. "Distribution of Expense Burden," *American Machinist*. May 25, 1911, pp. 991–94.

————, and Leon Pratt Alford. "The Principles of Management," *American Machinist* 36 (May 30, 1912), pp. 169–89.

Churchman, C. West. *The Design of Inquiring Systems*. New York: Basic Books, 1971.

Copley, F.B., and Frederick Taylor. *Father of Scientific Management*. New York and London: Harper and Bros., 1923, 2 vols.

Cyert, Richard M., and James March. *A Behavioral Theory of the Firm*. Englewood Cliffs, N.J.: Prentice-Hall, 1963.

Dale, Ernest. "Du Pont and Systematic Management," *Administrative Science Quarterly*. 1967. pp. 25–29.

————. "Contributions to Administration by Alfred P. Sloan, Jr. and GM," *Administrative Science Quarterly*. 1956, pp. 30–62.

Diemer, Hugo. "The Functions and Organization of the Purchasing Department," *Engineering Magazine* 18, 1900, p. 833.

Drucker, Peter F. *The Practice of Management*. New York: Harper, 1954.

Dunn, Edgar S., Jr. *Economic and Social Development: A Process of Social Learning*. Baltimore: Johns Hopkins Press, for Resources for the Future, 1971.

du Pont, Pierre S. "My Induction to Explosives Manufacture," The Papers of Pierre S. du Pont, the Eleutherian Mills Historical Library, Longwood Manuscripts, Group 10, Series B, File 5. Wilmington: 1945.

Emery, F.E., and E.L. Trist. "Casual Texture of Organizational Environments," *Human Relations* 18, August, 1962, pp. 20–26.

Fenwick, Noble James. "Organizational Management of New Knowledge: A Case Study of a State Bureaucracy." Doctoral dissertation, MIT, 1975.

Galbraith, Jay. *Designing Complex Organizations*. Reading, Mass.: Addison-Wesley, 1973.

Ginzburg, Eli. *The Human Economy*. New York: McGraw-Hill, 1976.

Haggerty, Patrick E. *Management Philosophies and Practices of Texas Instruments*. Texas Instruments, Inc., 1965.

————. "Objectives, Strategies, and Tactics." Annual Planning Conference, 1962.

————. "Innovation and the Private Enterprise System in the United States." Address before the National Academy of Engineering, April 24, 1968.

————. "Industrial Research and Development." Prepared for Rockefeller University Seminar on Science and the Evolution of Public Policy, March 16, 1972.

————. *The Productive Society.* New York: Columbia University Press, 1974.

Hofstede, G. H. *The Game of Budget Control.* London: Tavistock Publications, 1972.

Kerr, Steven. "On the Folly of Rewarding A, While Hoping for B," *Academy of Management Journal.* Vol. 18, December, 1975, pp. 769–83.

Kuhn, Arthur John. "An Application of a System Control Model to Business History: The General Motors Corporation Under Alfred P. Sloan," 1920–1935." Doctoral dissertation, University of California at Berkeley, 1972.

Kuhn, Thomas S. *The Structure of Scientific Revolutions.* 2d ed. Chicago: University of Chicago Press, 1970.

Lawrence, Paul R., and Jay Lorsch. *Organization and Environment.* Boston: Division of Research, Graduate School of Business, Harvard University, 1967.

Litterer, Joseph A. "Systematic Management: The Search for Order and Integration," *Business History Review* 35, Winter, 1961.

————. "Systematic Management: Design for Organizational Recoupling in American Manufacturing Firms," *Business History Review* 37, Winter, 1963.

————. *Analysis of Organizations*, 2nd ed. New York: Wiley, 1973.

————. "Alexander Hamilton Church and the Development of Modern Management," *Business History Review* 35, Summer, 1961, pp. 211–25.

————. "The Low Wages 'Boom'," *American Machinist*, Vol. 2, August 30, 1879.

March, James G., and Herbert Simon. *Organizations.* New York: Wiley, 1959.

McDonald, John. "What's Up—and Down—at Texas Instruments," *Fortune.* November 1961.

Metcalfe, Henry. *Cost Manufacturers and the Administration of Workshops, Public and Private*. New York: Wiley, 1885.

Murray, Edwin A. "The Implementation of Social Policies in Commercial Banks." D.B.A. dissertation, Graduate School of Business, Harvard University, 1974.

————. "The Social Response Process in Commercial Banks: An Empirical Investigation." *The Academy of Management Review*, Vol. 1, July, 1976.

Norman, Richard. "Organizational Innovativeness: Product Variation and Reorientation," *Administrative Science Quarterly*, June 1971.

Norris, H.M. "A Simple and Effective System of Shop Cost-Keeping." *Engineering Magazine* 16 (1898), p. 385.

————. "Shop System," *Iron Age* 54, November 1, 1894, p. 746.

Orcutt, H.F.L. "Machine Shop Management in Europe and America, VI. Comparisons as to Efficiency and Methods," *Engineering Magazine* 17, June 1899, p. 384.

Parsons, Talcott. *The Analysis of Organizations*, 2nd ed. New York: Wiley, 1973.

Perrow, Charles. "A Framework for the Comparative Analysis of Organizations," *American Sociological Review*, Vol. 32, 1967, pp. 194–208.

Phipps, Charles. "The IDEA Systems." Texas Instruments, Inc., June 1974.

————. "The OST System: A Management Approach to the Realization of Growth and Resource Goals." St. Louis, Mo., Sept. 9, 1975.

Popper, Karl. *Objective Knowledge*. Oxford: The Clarendon Press, 1972.

Rushing, William. "Hardness of Materials as Related to Division of Labor in Manufacturing Industries," *Administrative Science Quarterly* 13, 1968, pp. 229–45.

————. "Organizational Rules and Surveillance: Propositions in Comparative Organizational Analysis," *Administrative Science Quarterly* 10, March 1966, pp. 423–43.

Salter, Malcolm S. "Stages of Corporate Development," *Journal of Business Policy*, 1, 1970, pp. 23–37.

Schoenhof, J. *The Economy of High Wages*. New York: G.P. Putnam's Sons, 1893.

Scott, Bruce R. "Stages of Corporate Development," Parts I and II. Boston: Harvard Graduate School of Business, International Case Clearing House, #9-371-294 and 4-371-295.

Selznick, Phillip. *Leadership in Administration*. New York: Harper & Row, 1957.

Silverman, David. *The Theory of Organization: A Sociological Framework*. New York: Basic Books, 1971.

Simon, Herbert. *Administrative Behavior*. Second edition. New York: The Free Press, 1957.

Sloan, Alfred P., Jr. *My Years with General Motors*. Edited by John McDonald and Catherine Stevens. Garden City, N.Y.: Doubleday Anchor: 1972.

Smith, Adam. *An Inquiry into the Nature and Causes of The Wealth of Nations*. London: W. Strahan and T. Cadell, 1776.

Taylor, Frederick Winslow. *Shop Management*. New York: Harper, 1911.

Thompson, James D. *Organizations in Action*. New York: McGraw-Hill, 1967.

Tinkle, Long. *Mr De: A Biography of Everett Lee DeGolyer*. Boston: Little, Brown, 1970.

Tregoing, John. *A Treatise on Factory Management*. Lynn, Mass.: Press of T.P. Nichols, 1891.

Uyterhoeven, Hugo, Robert W. Ackerman, and John W. Rosenblum. *Strategy and Organization*. Homewood, Ill.: Irwin, 1973.

Van Gelder, Arthur Pine, and Hugo Schlatter. *History of the Explosives Industry in America*. New York: Columbia University Press, 1927.

Watzlawick, Paul, John Weakland, and Richard Risch. *Change: Principles of Problem Formation and Problem Resolution*. New York: W. W. Norton, 1974.

Weber, Max. *The Theory of Social and Economic Organization*. New York: The Free Press, 1964.

Wildavsky, Aaron. *The Politics of the Budgetary Process*. Second edition. Boston: Little, Brown, 1974.

"Works Management for the Maximum of Production: Organization as a Factor of Output," *Engineering Magazine*. 1899, p. 59.

Wren, Daniel A. *The Evolution of Management Thought*. New York: The Ronald Press, 1972.

INDEX

abstracted learning, xviii

action frame of reference, xiv

adaptation defined, xvii

administrative knowledge, xvii, 17, 152; as an administrative system, 155; as formally institutionalized learning, 155; as motivating the use of new knowledge, 155; as organizational learning, 150, 154

administrative systems, xx, xxi, 22, 42, 133, 148, 149, 152, 161; capture "knowledge about," 140; capture knowledge about coordinating tasks, 139; control information flow, 140; creating shared frame of reference, 139, 140; directing perception, 139; as a formal system, 64–65; focusing management attention, 140; focusing on patterns of thought, 139; focusing attention on pattern replication, 139; making knowledge accessible, 139, 156; making planning and policy possible, 139; as methodology for managing means of change, 139; must be consistent, 156; and OST as a system to decentralize strategic thinking, 148; and reasonable distinction between organizational learning and individual learning, 156; and rules for impounding new responses, 133; as a specified way of thinking about a specified class of situation, 133

adoption of knowledge, a human characteristic, xvii

Alford, Leon Pratt, 21; and Church, 21

American Machinist, 21

antitrust and Du Pont, 37

application of power to production, 6

Ashby, W. Ross, xvii

Babbage, Charles, 7, 10, 12–13

Barksdale, Hamilton, 34, 36

Baruch, Jordan J., xi

Bateson, Gregory, 141–43, 144

Beer, Stafford, 158

bounded rationality, xx

Brown, Donaldson, 40, 41–42, 139

Buckley, Walter, xix, 145

Bucy, Fred, 154

budgeting, xix

budgetary incrementalism, xviii

business objectives at Texas Instruments, 79–82

Chandler, Alfred D., Jr., xvi, 38; and Stephen Salsbury, 28

changes in the executive committee, 38–39

Church, Alexander Hamilton, xxi, 16–22, 25, 26–27, 133, 145; and Leon Pratt Alford, 21; concerned with the ongoing business of the firm as a whole, 140; his accounting methods as guide for management thought, 138; and Taylor, their systematic management, contributions, 22

commercial applications, as aim of TI's goods-directed research, 77

complexity, xv, xix, 5, 9, 16, 32, 135

consistency, as a key of success, 154

control of innovation, a criterion in relation to milestones, 116; by negotiation, 114

coordination, 5

Corporate Development Committee at Texas Instruments, 89, 90, 104, 115–16, 117, 151; and role in prioritizing OST positions, 114–18

Corporate-level Committees at Texas Instruments, 101–07

creative backlog, 89

cultural "congruence" as possibly imperative to significant planning, 161

Cyert, Richard M., 11; and James G. March, 50, 136, 138, 143–44, 148, 161

Degolyer, Everette Lee, 52

Development Department at Du Pont, 37–38

development of management thought, 5

digital analysis of seismic data, 62–63

diversity in markets, xvi, 34–38

diversity in products, xvi, 37–38, 43–44

division of labor, 7, 15

division of managerial labor, 15, 17

Du Pont Corporation, xv, xx–xxi, 3, 25, 27, 32, 34, 133, 146, 158; administrative systems divide performance and coordination, 138, 140; makes synergy possible, 138; excess capacity of, 38; executive committee of, 34, 35, 36, 37, 41; financial controls of, 34–35; functional department structure proposed by Moxham, 34; in financial panic of 1907–08, 35; management controls of, 34, 138; new administrative structure of, 32; new consolidation strategy of, 29–32; Operative Committee of, 36; and purchase of old company, 1902, 29; reorganization of 1911, 36

du Pont, Alfred I., 27

du Pont, Col. Henry, 27, 42

du Pont, Lammot, 27

du Pont, Pierre S. 27–34, 39–40, 41

du Pont, T. Coleman, 27–34

Durant, William G., 39

Emerson, Harrington, 21

Emery, F.E., and E.L. Trist, xi, xix

Engineering Magazine, 6

Fenwick, Noble James: defines hierarchies of learning, 142

financial controls at Du Pont, 1971–73, 34–35

financial controls at General Motors, 40–42; as a base for policy decisions, 45

financial controls, to monitor results, 41–42

frame of reference, xiv, xv, 136, 139, 140, 147, 157

Ford, Henry, 45

General Motors, xvi, xxi, 3, 27, 39, 133, 146, 158; administrative systems divide performance and coordination of, 138; in crisis of 1924, 44; and change, 44; Executive Committee of, 41–42; financial controls of, 40–42, 44, 45; and forecasts for control, 44; management controls made possible synergy, 138

Geophysical Services, Inc., 51–54

germanium transistors, 60

Galbraith, Jay, 21

goal-directed research: as essential for successful innovation, 78; as outcome of tight coupling, 78, 90–98

Haggerty, Patrick E., xxi–xxii, 50, 51, 53–56, 58, 61–62, 64–65, 69, 71, 74–79, 93, 98, 125, 146–49, 151–53, 155

hardness of material, 7

hard technology, 6

hierarchy, xvi, 43

hierarchy of goals at Texas Instruments, 79–83

hierarchy of learning, 141–43, 145, 157

higher level learning, 142–45

high volume production, 5, 13

I*D*E*A system, The, 150–51; as an alternative access route, 151; as variant of the original OST, 150, 152

incrementalism, xix

individual in contrast to organizational

ment, 78; means to focus attention of senior management, 101; means of innovation in general, 101; its methodology as means to integrate P&AE with an ongoing business, 126; monitoring it as based on unspecified parameters, 155; required changes in, 93; requires top-level involvement, 153; review and control, 89–91; substantially refined since inception, 153; system to replicate strategic thinking, 98; systemizing "tight coupling," 148–59; top-level management backing, 100; way of thinking, 101

operating mode, 83

organic functional areas, 18

organizational climate, xv, 158–61

organizational learning, xii, xiii, xvi, xvii, xviii, xxii, 133, 136, 143; abstraction based, 144; adaptation or change of the patterns themselves, 156; application of successful patterns to new or changed situations, 156; communications phenomenon, 142–43; 161; contrast to individual learning, 142; contrast to "mere adaptation," 142; criteria to define, 142; definition as nonexhaustive, 156; distinguishing between individual and organizational learning, 156; distinguishing between learning and "mere adaptation," 156; evidence for, 161; function of general principle, 146; functioning of a shared frame of reference, 142; generalized insight, 144; insights accessible to others, 156; institutionalized understanding, 100; "knowledge about" the administrative system, 100; "learning rules," 144, 156

organizational learning, replication as evidence for, 136; requiring a shared frame of reference, 99, 144

overhead expenses, 20

paradigm, 147

paradigm change: creating a shared frame of reference, 147; generalized insight, 147; high-level learning, 146–48; institutionalizing individual insights, 147; purposeful strategy, 148

Parsons, Talcott, 158

People and Asset Effectiveness (P&AE), 49, 104, 151; application of OST methods, 125; committee, 104, 123, 124; compared to OST and PCC, 122; defined, 119; "discretionary expenditure," 119; generalized form of OST, 101, 119; goal directed effort, 119; impact of, 126; judged against milestones, 119; means to tap synergies of innovation, 125; measured system, 122; modelled on OST experience, 122–27; productivity, 122; top-level backing, 122–24

polystable environment, xix

pocket radio, 61

Politics of the Budgetary Process (1964), xviii

Popper, Karl, xvii

power, 8

Pratt, John, 40

precision, 7, 8

predictability, xviii, 5; essential to systematic management, 145

process of budget setting, xix

processes in product, xv–xvi

Product-Customer Center (PCC), 65–69, 141, 157; balance in the ongoing business, 140; as basis of operating structure at TI, 65–69; as focus for routine activities at TI, 69; hierarchical system of, 66; and innovation, 75; and need for formal integration, 74; operating mode of, in contrast to OST's strategic mode, 83; as the fundamental operating structure, 79;

ABOUT THE AUTHOR

MARIANN JELINEK, Assistant Professor of Business Administration at the Amos Tuck School at Dartmouth College, is a specialist on administrative systems innovation. Professor Jelinek's research centers on administrative systems as means of organizational control and guidance, particularly for innovation.

Prior to joining the Tuck School, Professor Jelinek taught at Worcester Polytechnic Institute and Bentley College. She studied at the Graduate School of Business, Harvard University, where she received her D.B.A. degree in 1977 as one of the first graduates in the administrative systems program. Her dissertation, on Texas Instruments, is the basis for the present study. Dr. Jelinek also holds a Ph.D. from the University of California at Berkeley.

RELATED TITLES
Published by
Praeger Special Studies